American Christmas Stories

Volume 1

A collection of true Christmas stories, letters, and customs from American history

Compiled by
Nicki Truesdell

Copyright 2023
Knowledge Keepers Bookstore
ISBN: 979-8-9886361-2-0

Table of contents

a

Introduction

America is still a young country, and our history of Christmas celebrations reflects this. Though we now have some fairly universal customs, such as Christmas lights on the house, our favorite Christmas movies with hot cocoa, busy shopping, and holiday travel, it wasn't that long ago that our ancestors across the country had widely differing celebrations.

While the settled families on the east coast were enjoying Christmas dinner and gift giving, their pioneer friends and relatives out west might be huddled in a freezing cabin or other crude shelter, happy with a fresh deer and some warm bread. As the civilization spread westward over 200 years, the luxuries of holiday celebrations were quite diverse.

The history of Christmas celebrations in America was not always like the quaint Victorian-era Christmas cards would have us believe. When settlers first came to these shores, Christmas was more of a religious holiday observance than a big celebration. The Puritans at Plymouth did not celebrate the day; they worked in the fields instead. It went against their strict Puritan beliefs. As the day became a more acceptable holiday, it was often observed with a large meal, visiting nearby friends, firing weapons, and a church service.

As the country became more connected through railroad travel and telegraph communication, customs began to be more cohesive. America was becoming its own culture. By the mid 1800s, more and more Christmas customs gained in popularity, and grew into the popular Christmas culture of the 20th century.

The country's first Christmas tree reportedly was displayed in the 1830s. The Christmas tree's popularity spread with the help of the influential magazine *Godey's Lady's Book*, which in 1850 published the 1848 illustration of the British royals, though the depiction of the family was altered to appear American. This and other efforts helped make Christmas trees popular in the United States by the 1870s.[1] Trees were simply decorated with nuts, strings of popcorn or beads, oranges, lemons, candies, and candles.

The first American Christmas card was distributed in the 1850s. You can read more about that in this book. In another section, you'll get a sense of Christmas dinners that are quite different from what we are accustomed to in the 21st century. The rise of gift-giving began in the 1870s, as well as charitable giving during this holiday season.

The stories in this book are all true, as is the custom of Knowledge Keepers. They range in date from 1773 to 1926, from the big city to the

---

[1] Britannica

western outpost. Each story is short enough to be read in a brief moment of relaxation throughout the holiday season, taking you back to celebrations as varied as our patchwork past.

I hope you thoroughly enjoy these little tidbits of history as you enjoy your modern Christmas celebrations, and perhaps find a little something in these pages to bring into your family traditions.

Merry Christmas,

Nicki Truesdell,
Founder, Knowledge Keepers Bookstore
December 2023

Address at the 150th Anniversary

of the Battles of Trenton and Princeton

Trenton, N.J.

CALVIN COOLIDGE
30th President of the United States:
1923 - 1929

*This is a different kind of Christmas
address from a United States President,
but it is included in this volume because
of its passion for the principles that drove
Washington and his men through some
very difficult Christmas nights.*

December 29, 1926

Fellow Countrymen:

The season is now well advanced in the celebrations of the one hundred and fiftieth anniversary of the opening events of the American Revolution. The year of 1925 marked the passage of a century and a half of time from the days of Lexington, Concord, and Bunker Hill, and the assumption by Washington of the post of Commander in Chief of the Continental Army at Cambridge. During the following March of 1776 in forcing the British to evacuate Boston he secured his first military success. In the following July the Declaration of Independence was adopted by the Continental Congress at Philadelphia. The early summer saw nearly 30,000 British, under the command of Sir William Howe, landed at Staten Island. Coming in contact with some of these forces on Long Island and again at White Plains, the Americans fought without success. But General Washington was entitled to great credit for extricating his Army, which was then forced for nearly two months to retreat through New Jersey, and crossing the Delaware at Trenton reached the Pennsylvania shore December 8 barely in time to escape from Cornwallis.

Although the Americans were safe for the moment, as they had possession of all the boats up and down the river for 70 miles, their situation was so desperate that Washington thought it might be necessary to retreat into Virginia, or even go beyond the Alleghenies. All hope of taking Canada was gone. New York had been lost. The British had advanced into New Jersey. Even the Congress had fled from Philadelphia to Baltimore. Intrenched behind the Delaware with a ragged, starving army, poorly equipped, broken in morale, dwindling through the expiration of enlistments and daily desertions, while the patriotic cause was at its lowest ebb, on December 18 Washington wrote to his brother:

> *You can form no idea of the perplexity of my situation. No man, I believe, ever had a greater choice of difficulties and less means to extricate himself from them. However, under a full persuasion of the justice of our cause I can not entertain an idea that it will finally sink, though it may remain for some time under a cloud.*

There you have the full measure of the Father of his Country. He faced the facts; He recognized the full import of their seriousness. But he was firm in the faith that the right would prevail. To faith he proposed to add works. If ever a great cause depended for its success on one man, if ever a mighty destiny was identified with one person in these dark and despondent hours, that figure was Washington.

Such was the prelude to the historic events which, notwithstanding their discouraging beginning, were soon to culminate in the brilliant victories of the patriotic armies in the Battles of Trenton and Princeton, the one hundred and fiftieth anniversary of which the people of New Jersey are now so appropriately celebrating. After a series of engagements and retreats which can only be characterized as defeats, running from April to late December, Washington now decided to take the offensive. While some of his generals supported this proposal, others were doubtful. Colonel Stark, who was to be heard from at the Battle of Bennington in the following August, is reported to have advised the commander in chief as follows:

> *Your men have too long been accustomed to place their dependence for safety upon spades and pickaxes. If you ever expect to establish the independence of these States, you must teach them to place dependence upon their firearms and courage.*

It was finally decided to attempt the crossing of the Delaware from Pennsylvania into New Jersey on Christmas night, 1776, for the purpose of a surprise attack on the Hessians who occupied Trenton. Orders were issued to Colonel Cadwalader, commanding three Philadelphia battalions, to cross at Bristol, and

4

to General Ewing, of the Pennsylvania Militia, to cross at Trenton Ferry. Washington planned to take his army over at McKonkeys Ferry. The crossing has ever since been well-known history. The cold, the sleet, the wind, the great cakes of floating ice made the effort well-nigh impossible. But for the skill of a regiment of fishermen from Marblehead, Massachusetts, under the command of Colonel Glover, the effort would have failed. The commands of Cadwalader and Ewing were unable to reach the New Jersey shore. Tradition relates that Washington said to General Knox: "The fate of an empire depends upon this night." It was not until 4 o'clock in the morning that the little army of 2,500 men began their march on Trenton. The password was "Victory or death." The storm of sleet was freezing as it fell, the mud was deep, the night was dark. Being told the muskets were too wet to use, Washington continued the advance and ordered that where gunpowder failed the bayonets be used.

About 8 o'clock the Americans emerging through the storm surprised the Hessians at Trenton, then a village of about 800 inhabitants, killed their commander, Colonel Rall, and captured between 1,000 and 1,500 men. It is said that Washington personally directed the artillery fire. Alexander Hamilton commanded a battery. Being unsupported and outnumbered three to one, Washington recrossed the

Delaware and again took up his position on the Pennsylvania shore.[2]

It can not be said that this ranks as a great battle, but it was the turning point in the Revolutionary War at which defense and defeat became offense and victory. From that hour the spirit of the patriot cause rose. The inhabitants of this region began to remove their loyalist flags and to manifest their open adherence to the American cause. Early on New Year morning Robert Morris was busy waking people in Philadelphia making appeals for money to support the army. He secured $50,000, which went largely to pay the soldiers, encouraging them to remain after their enlistments had expired.

Meanwhile Cadwalader had crossed the Delaware. Learning of his movements, on the 30th Washington again occupied Trenton and drew his lines on the south side of Assunpink Creek with about 5,000 men. Skirmishers which he sent toward Princeton were driven back by the British commanded by Cornwallis, who encamped on the north banks of the creek, expecting with his superior numbers to overwhelm the Americans on the following day. Realizing that he could not recross the Delaware for lack of boats and that his army was too weak to advance, Washington held a midnight council

---

[2] See *War in the Colonies: The Life of George Washington Volume 2* by John Marshall at Knowledge Keepers Bookstore

at which it was decided to leave their camp fires burning and their sentinels posted while the army moved off to the right and marched rapidly around behind the British position. Just after daybreak Cornwallis heard the roar of Washington's guns from Princeton, a dozen miles away, where a sharp engagement took place. When the battalions of Mercer and Cadwalader were thrown into disorder Washington rode to the front, rallied his men, and brought victory out of defeat. Having routed the British, he continued north toward Brunswick, but finding his men too exhausted to attack the British depot turned his army north toward Morristown, where he arrived on January 7.

By this brilliant action he had broken through the lines of General Howe and held a position where he could recruit his army and continue the war. "Earlier successes," says John Fiske, "had been local. This was continental. Seldom has so much been done with such slender means." On hearing what Washington had accomplished, Sir Horace Walpole wrote, "His march through our lines is allowed to have been a prodigy of generalship. In one word, I took upon a great part of America as lost to this country." After this display of valor and success, Congress hastened to vote more troops and supplies. Recruits began to arrive. The crisis was passed. The way was open to arouse the spirit of the Colonies to such point that they were able in the following October to surround and defeat Burgoyne at Saratoga. That victory brought the open support of France and led on to Yorktown and independence.

It is the relationship of events which makes them important. The capture of a small outpost in a little village by the Revolutionary force of scarcely 2,500 men is not in itself impressive. The night march from the south side of Assunpink, the surprise attack on Princeton, the escape of the patriot army through the British lines, hold a rather trifling place if considered merely as a military achievement. The colonists had demonstrated that they could fight at Bunker Hill. But that was more than a year and a half ago, and it was not a victory. Washington had demonstrated his military capacity by the successful and almost bloodless siege of Boston. He had shown his strategy in the retreat from Long Island. But here at last he had led an attack of great boldness, had one or two actions in the field, and finally reached his objective. This was successful offensive victory. He had demonstrated his genius for command. His cause was far from won. He was yet to pass that terrible winter at Valley Forge and meet the shock of Arnold's treachery on the Hudson. But hereafter he stood out as a general that commanded the pride of his countrymen and the respect of their foes. Thereafter everyone knew that the Colonies had an army in the field that would fight and could win victories. It was that knowledge and that army which were the entire support of the Revolutionary movement.

We can not, however, put the main emphasis of these important events on their immediate results. It was not that they enthused the patriots with a new spirit which enabled them to win important victories in the coming campaigns of 1777. The war could have been lost many times in the following years. It was not even the more distant day of independence. A straggling, dissevered, unrelated aggregation of Colonies, each a prey alike to its own domestic jealousies and foreign intrigue, riotous, impotent, bankrupt, would scarcely have been worth the blood and treasure expended for a nominal and fleeting independence. The American Revolution was not an accomplished fact until the adoption of our Federal Constitution and the establishment under its provisions of an efficiently functioning government. Unless the engagements at Trenton and Princeton had led in his direction, they would have been all in vain and we should not be here assembled to do our reverence to them and their heroic figures.

Washington and his generals are gone. The bloody tracks which their barefoot armies often left on the frozen ground have long since been washed away. The smoke of the conflict in which they engaged has cleared. The civil strife and disorder which followed have been dissipated. But the institutions which they founded, the Government which they established, have not only remained, but have grown in strength and importance and extended their influence throughout the earth. We can never go to their assistance with supplies and reinforcements. We can never lend our counsel to their political deliberations. But we can support the Government and institutions which are their chief titles to the esteem and reverence in which they are held by the common consent of all humanity.

Our country has traveled far since these soul-inspiring days. Our progress has been great. Our prosperity has been the wonder of the world. Our present-day existence has its difficulties, requiring courage and resourcefulness. The political and economic life of the Nation offers abundant opportunity for developing the character and increasing the moral power of the people. I believe it to be a grave error to assert that the spiritual force of the men and women of the Revolutionary period was superior to that which exists in the America of the present. But they did set for us an example which no nation can ignore and long exist. No doubt their desire was as great as ours, if their chance to gratify it was more limited, for an opportunity to reap a profit from following their own business and living in security and peace. But this was not their supreme choice. They were willing to accord to those rights which they set out in the Declaration of Independence something more than lip service. When they had pledged to the support of those principles their lives, their fortunes, and their sacred honor, they demonstrated by their actions that they stood ready to redeem that pledge. In order that their ideals might be maintained, they did not hesitate to sacrifice all that they had and were.

The Colonies of those days had little in the way of accumulated wealth, but by hard work the people on the whole maintained themselves in comfort. Those conditions, as everyone knows, have been radically changed. Through the development of our natural resources, our inventive genius, and mechanical skill this Nation has become possessed of very large wealth. Such a situation has its dangers. In past history it has usually led first to luxury and ease and later to decline and decay. We do not yet appear to be tending in that direction. While we have a considerable extent of what might be called luxury, it is not of that destructive nature which has in the past afflicted other people. In a wide measure it is for use rather than display. It makes its appeal to the soul rather than to the senses. With whatever else we may be charged, our sharpest critics do not claim that this is a nation given over to ease. The fact is that idleness is no longer fashionable. The American of large possessions has not been afflicted with indolence. Rather, he has been a victim of overstrain and overwork. The class of idle rich in this country has dwindled to such small proportions that it is no longer worth noticing. No doubt it can be said that we have permitted certain types of extravagance, as in the use of our natural resources and in the waste that attends the conduct of much of our daily life, but as a nation it does not appear that we are suffering any impairment through a spread of luxury and ease.

The main effort of our Revolutionary period, it seems to me, was to bestow upon the individual a larger freedom guaranteed by the authority of law. When the battles were over and the Federal Constitution with its Bill of Rights had been adopted, when the Federal courts had been appointed and the jurisdiction of the national laws was thoroughly established, the people of this country found themselves in the possession of greater liberties than were enjoyed by any other nation. While our political ideals were in many respects an inheritance, and our political capacity the result of generations of experience, our theory and form of a representative system of self-government based on the broad doctrine of equality, recognizing that the individual had rights upon which not even the Government itself could encroach, was something altogether new in the world. It completely obliterated the old system of class and caste and opened wide the door of opportunity to every talent. What had heretofore been the privilege of the few immediately became the right of the many. Under the great intellectual and spiritual awakening which this new conception of human relationship brought about the Nation began that rapid development and expansion which has been so continuous and increasing through the whole length of our history. Our fears in the end have proved to be delusions, while it has been our hopes that have proved to be realities,

We have wondered whether a people left entirely to themselves with no restraints except those which were self-imposed through their own political action would be able to exercise sufficient self-control to remain economically sound. We have wondered whether there would be enough security for property against confiscatory action, so that there could be sufficient accumulations of capital to finance the needs of a rapidly expanding nation with its many requirements for tremendous investments, to provide it with the necessary methods of production and distribution. We have seen that under a republic, with the great inspiration that it gives to private initiative, our accomplishments in this direction have surpassed those of any other country. We have wondered whether, if the individual were left unrestricted, and more intelligent, more resourceful, and more unscrupulous would not gather unto themselves so large a proportion of the wealth of the country that they would dominate the great mass of the people by the mere weight and power of money. But some way people of that stamp do not prosper, do not gain real power. We have seen many great fortunes accumulated. But they do not dominate the people. Rather the people dominate them. Their whole tendency has been toward investment for the benefit of the public. Some of those which stood out as the largest scarcely 25 years ago have been practically all bestowed upon charity, while men at that time obscure and unknown have risen to the highest rank in the wealth of our country. Who can doubt that these results are even now in the process of repetition? As a general rule with us great wealth has meant great public service.

We have only look about us to see that under our institutions these conditions, instead of affording a means of burdening and oppressing the great mass of the people, have rather afforded them means for a higher standard of living and greater degree of prosperity than ever before existed. Under our system, the wealth of the country instead of tending to concentration tends to distribution. If all the large fortunes in the country were combined, their amount in comparison with our entire wealth would not be large. The fact is that the great mass of the property of the country is owned by the people of the country. This is the great outstanding fact in the economic life of America. It can not be too often stated or too strongly emphasized. Instead of retarding, our political institutions have advanced and strengthened our economic condition.

We are placing a great deal of emphasis on prosperity. Our people ought to desire to be prosperous, but it ought not to be their main desire. There are other things that they ought to want more. Prosperity is not a cause; it is a result. It is not based on indolence and ease, on avarice and greed, or on selfishness and self-indulgence. It is the result of industry, fair dealing, self-denial, and generosity. It is all summed up in a single word. It is character. If the country will put its emphasis on this process and remember to practice these virtues its prosperity will become greater and greater, and the greater it becomes the more worthy it will be of our admiration. A more efficient service, one to another, will be the foundation of a greater prosperity and of a stronger national character.

It is never possible to discuss the political institutions which resulted from the American Revolution without realizing that their fundamental conception is reliance on the individual. The whole system of a self-supporting, self-governing people breaks down both in theory and in practice unless the individual is of a character capable of rising to the great dignity of that position. The whole record of American success is traceable to the excellence of American citizenship. To such a people institutions, of course, are important. Our political organization with its representative system and its local self-government, its strong executive authority and independent courts, harmonizes our historical background with sound, social principles. Yet this elaborate and well-wrought out system would be of little avail unless the people supply sufficient energy and intelligence to make it work. Unless that be done, there is no system of government that can supply a nation with political salvation. Under our theory, the citizen is sovereign. Whenever he abdicates, some pretender assumes the throne. In large centers of population this has often taken the form of what we term a political boss. The voters cease to function in their sovereign capacity and turn their power over to some individual who rules in their stead. They cease thinking and acting for themselves and permit some one to think and act for them. They are not willing to make the sacrifice and perform the service which is necessary to support self-government.

When this condition exists, there may be many palliatives but there is only one fundamental remedy. Methods can be devised under which it may be more difficult for the political dictator to remain in power and more easy for the great body of the voters to direct their own destiny. But under our institutions the only way to perfect our government is to perfect the individual citizen. It is necessary to reach the mind and the soul of the individual. It is not merely a change of environment but a change of heart that is needed. The power of the law may help, but only the power of righteousness can be completely sufficient. I know of no way that this can be done save through the influences of religion and education. By religion I do not mean either fanaticism or bigotry; by education I do not mean the cant of the schools; but a broad and tolerant faith, loving thy neighbor as thyself, and a training and experience that enables the human mind to see into the heart of things. This has been a long, slow, and laborious process, accompanied by many failures and many disappointments. No doubt there will be many more in the future. But those who have faith in the power of the individual to work toward moral perfection are willing to entrust their destiny to that method of reform. It is that faith which justifies the American conception of popular sovereignty. There is no other theory by which we could explain the making of the American Nation and no other theory on which we can hope for its continuity. It was in this faith that Washington crossed the Delaware.

It is true that the world is coming to comprehend the spirit of service better than it ever did before. We ought to rejoice in that conception. But that theory does not run counter to the theory of independence. The Colonies had been called on to fight the European wars on this side of the Atlantic. They had been required to pay tribute to liquidate European debts and support the European military establishment. They had been forced to submit to the regulation and control of their trade for the benefit of European commerce. They determined to resist these unjust impositions and establish their complete independence. They did not then and do not now fail to recognize that they are a part of the civilized world, and that they owe not only to themselves but to others great obligations. But they were determined then and are determined now to be the masters of their own destiny and the judges of their own conduct. They knew, and we ought to know, that unless we can be American we can not be anything. Unless we look after ourselves we can not look after anybody else. The obligations of civilization are reciprocal. The same consideration that we owe to others they owe to us.

Washington and the patriots of his day wanted peace. We want peace. They found it was necessary to make great sacrifices in order to secure it. We can not escape the corresponding sacrifices, sometimes for the purpose of providing adequate national defense, sometimes through international covenants by limiting the scope of our military forces. I do not believe we can advance the policy of peace by a return to the policy of competitive armaments. While I favor an adequate army and navy, I am opposed to any effort to militarize this Nation. When that method has been worked out to its logical consequences the result has always been a complete failure. We can render no better service to humanity than to put forth all our influence to prevent the world from slipping back into the grasp of that ravaging system. Truth and faith and justice have a power of their own in which we are justified in placing a very large reliance. Washington could carry on the war because, as he wrote to his brother, he had "a full persuasion of the justice of our cause." It was the final conviction on the part of the British that their cause was not just that led them to abandon their attempt to subdue the Colonies.

In nations, individuals have their counterpart. As we can expect some help from domestic laws, so we can expect some help from international covenants. While each represents the best that humanity can do at this time, neither in themselves are sufficient. As it is necessary to change the heart of the individual, so it is necessary to change the hearts of nations. This has often been referred to as moral disarmament. The mistake that is being made in application lies in the fact that it does not its come first. If the world had complete change of heart, complete moral disarmament, complete mutual understanding, complete sympathy, we would have little need of armaments and no need at all for international treaties limiting their use and size. It is because all nations are in danger from this source that we ought to provide such artificial barriers as are possible for the protection of the peace and welfare of humanity. It is because the spirit of avarice, of jealousy, of hate and revenge are not yet eliminated from the hearts of the nations that it is well for them to take counsel together that they may devise means for protecting themselves from these evil counselors, that they may deliver themselves from their control and come more completely under the dominion of benevolence kindliness, charitableness, and good will. Altogether too much of international relationship is based on fear. Nations rejoice in the fact that they have the courage to fight each other. When will the time come that they have the courage to trust each other?

The world has been striving to advance in this direction, to discard the old theory of relying entirely on force and to adopt the method of relying more on reason. We are in danger of slipping back into the old formula. The habit and tradition of ages call us in that direction. We can not establish the new principle unless we are willing to make some sacrifices, unless we are willing to put some courage into our convictions. We have met to celebrate some of the events which secured our independence. I believe we are strong enough and brave enough to resist another domination of the world by the military spirit through our own independent action. This is the holy season. All humanity has laid aside the burdens of the day that they might rejoice in the glad tidings of "Peace on earth, good will toward men." Remembering the sacrifices of Washington and his patriot army endured for us, we ought not to shrink from sacrifice to make that inspired vision a practical reality.

Christmas Musings

By
Susan Fenimore Cooper

1848

Susan Fenimore Cooper was the
daughter of famed author James
Fenimore Cooper (Leatherstocking
Tales). She was a naturalist and activist
in the early 19th century. The following
Christmas musings are from her diary,
which was later published as *Rural
Hours.*

December 21-

It is snowing a little, we may yet have
sleighing for Christmas. It is a very busy
time within doors. For the activity in the
rural housekeeper's department is now at
its height. A variety of important labors
connected with Christmas cheer are going
on. Cake jars are filling up with crullers,
flat, brown and crisp; with dough-nuts,
dark, full and round; and raisined
olecokes. Waffles, soft and hard, make
their appearance on the tea tables; mince-
pies, with their heavy freight of rich
materials, are getting underway; and
cranberries are preparing for
tarts. Calves'-head soup and calves'-foot
jellies are under consideration; turkeys
and ducks are fattening in the poultry
yard while inquiries are made after game
birds and fish from the lake. There is a
dawn of the kindliness and good-will
belonging to Christmas perceptible in the
kitchen and pantry; the eggs are beaten
more briskly, the sugar and butter are
stirred more readily, and the mince-meat
chopped more heartily than on any other
occasion during the year.

Greens are put up in some houses. And, of course, Santa Claus must also be looked after. Santa's pouch and pack must be well filled for the little people, with this or that nursery-book, sugar-plums and candies, puppets and toys...such as those huge babies of cotton and linen with pretty painted faces, and soft, supple limbs. The rag-babies or, more properly, *Moppets*, are always pets with little mammas, for no other dolls are loved so dearly as these. But it is not just adult women who make Christmas presents; many little slips of womankind are now busily engaged upon some nice piece of work, with bags, purses, slippers, mittens, what-nots all getting a more finished look every hour.

December 22-

We shall doubtless have sleighing for the holidays.

December 23-

Winter is out in its true colors at last. It is a picture postcard day. Merry bells are jingling through the village streets. There are cutters and sleighs with gay parties dashing rapidly about. It is well for Santa Clause that we have snow,

if we may believe Mr. Clement Clark
Moore, who has seen him nearer than most
people, he travels in a miniature sleigh
with eight tiny rein-deer.

December 25-

Christmas must always be a happy,
cheerful day, for even when the sky is
cloudy and dull, the bright fires, the fresh
and fragrant greens, the friendly gifts, and
words of good-will, the 'Merry Christmas'
smiles, create a warm glow and humble
backdrop for the exalted associations of the
festival, as it is celebrated in solemn,
public worship, and kept by the hearts of
believing Christians. Other religions have
scarcely heeded children, yet Christianity
bestows on them an especial blessing. The
unfeigned, unalloyed gayety of children
makes Christmas merry.

Christmas on a Virginia Plantation

1773

From

Virginia Tutor: Journal of Phillip Vickers Fithian
1773-1774

Published by Knowledge Keepers
Bookstore

Saturday December 25, 1773

I was waked this morning by Guns fired all
round the House. The morning is stormy, the
wind at South East rains hard. Nelson the Boy
who makes my Fire, blacks my shoes, does
errands &c. was early in my Room, drest only in
his shirt and Breeches! He made me a vast fire,
blacked my Shoes, set my Room in order, and
wish'd me a joyful Christmas, for which I gave
him half a Bit.—Soon after he left the Room, and
before I was Drest, the Fellow who makes the
Fire in our School Room, drest very neatly in
green, but almost drunk, entered my chamber
with three or four profound Bows, & made me
the same salutation; I gave him a Bit, and
dismissed him as soon as possible.—Soon after
my Cloths and Linen were sent in with a message
for a Christmas Box, as they call it; I sent the
poor Slave a Bit, & my thanks.—I was obliged
for want of small change, to put off for some
days the Barber who shaves & dresses me.—I
gave Tom the Coachman, who Doctors my
Horse, for his care two Bits, & am to give more
when the Horse is well.—I gave to Dennis the
Boy who waits at Table half a Bit—So that the
sum of my Donations to the Servants, for this
Christmas appears to be five Bits, a Bit is a
pisterene bisected; or an English sixpence, &
passes here for seven pence Halfpenny, the whole
is *3s 1½d.*—

At Breakfast, when Mr Carter entered the
Room, he gave us the compliments of the Season.
He told me, very civilly, that as my Horse was
Lame, his own riding Horse is at my Service to
ride when & where I Choose.

Mrs Carter was, as always, cheerful, chatty, &
agreeable; She told me after Breakfast several
droll, merry Occurrences that happened while she
was in the City Williamsburg.—

This morning came from the Post-office at
Hobbes-Hole, on the Rappahannock, our News-
papers. Mr Carter takes the Pennsylvania Gazette,
which seems vastly agreeable to me, for it is like
having something from home—But I have yet no
answer to my Letter. We dined at four o-Clock—
Mr Carter kept in his Room, because he
breakfasted late, and on Oysters—There were at
Table Mrs Carter & her five Daughters that are at
School with me—
Miss Priscilla, Nancy, Fanny, Betsy, and Harriot,
five as beautiful delicate, well-instructed
Children as I have ever known!—Ben is
abroad; Bob & Harry are out; so there was no
Man at Table but myself.—I must carve—Drink
the Health—and talk if I can! Our Dinner was no
otherwise than common, yet as elegant
a Christmas Dinner as I ever sat Down to—The
table Discourse was Marriage;
Mrs Carter observ'd that was she a Widow, she
should scruple to marry any man alive; She gave
a reason, that She did not think it probable a man

could love her grown old when the world is
thronged with blooming, ripening Virgins; but in
fact Mrs Carter looks & would pass for a younger
Woman than some unmarried Ladies of my
acquaintance, who would willingly enough make
us place them below twenty!—We dined at four;
when we rose from table it was growing dark—
The wind continues at South East & is stormy
and muddy.

(The custom of firing powder during the Christmas season is
one that persists in the South today in various forms.)

Christmas in Chicago

1926

BY FANNY BUTCHER

Fanny Butcher was a journalist and literary critic in for the Chicago Tribune from 1923-1963. She was well known to the famous authors of her time, including Earnest Hemingway.

CHRISTMAS IN CHICAGO

1926

BY FANNY BUTCHER

A FLARE of lights. A giant tree tapering up and up until it seems to melt into the sky, except that the glittering star which crowns it puts to shame the gentle glimmerings in the background of the blue-black heavens. Spangles, like a circus-rider's dress, flutter in the swish of air, blaze out in the footlight glare of the barrage of lights which are turned on the tree. The family Christmas tree giganticized to a tree for the family of the great city.

And underneath, thousands upon thousands of human beings tramping about in the snow, listening to a band, watching the fluttering bangles of the spectacular tree. A river of motors slowly flowing past the picture–slowly, whether they will or no, for there is no hurrying in the mass that drives down to see the tree.

In the mêlée that worms about beneath the tree there are men and women from the four corners of the earth. There are faces moulded in such fantastically different casts that you cannot but wonder how mankind can be all one mankind. There are voices thick with the gutturals of Middle Europe, soft with the sunshine of the South, and heavy with the interminable consonants of the North.

There is a medley of sound, human voices of all the tones of the earth's surface doing that peculiarly unmusical feat of all talking at once, and being heightened rather than subdued by the din of the band trying to be heard in a bellowing of that gentle lullaby 'Heilige Nacht.'[3] And the overtone is always the honking of impatient motorists or gayly inclined ones who feel that the best way to express approval in modern life is to make as loud and raucous a noise as possible.

And all over the city, in its endless miles of boulevards and parks, little brothers of the great tree are glittering against the sky. And underneath those others, as underneath the great tree itself, mankind swishes and huddles and gazes and talks. Miles and miles apart they are, from the steel mills on the south painting the sky a flame red to the fastnesses of suburban sobriety and sedateness on the north, from the vast new bungalow-studded southwest to the factory-dotted northwest merging into two-flat buildings and inter-urbaned real estate plots.

The municipal tree of Chicago—whether it be the great tree on the lake front or the offspring

---

[3] Silent Night

which each local community rears as a pledge of its own Christmas joys–is a triumph of civic ideals. It is a symbol to the thousands, who are strangers–if not in fact, at least in that pitifully intense way in which mankind can be alone in the millions that make a great city–that the city is human. And it has been such a short time that the city has been human–that it has had time to be anything but a growing, hungry, physically developing giant of a child. Out of its rompers, Chicago is now, and present at the great moment of decorating the Christmas tree of the 'children.'

The Municipal Christmas tree in Chicago, circa 1913. (Chicago History Museum)

There is something adolescent and very charming and very *naïve* about this Christmasy Chicago. It has just reached the time when it feels that the world is taking some notice of it, when it feels its first thrills of conquest, when it cleans out its pockets, throws away the broken

knife blades and the slightly worn wads of gum
and the marbles and substitutes the picture of
the chorus girl and the pocket comb. It is
washing behind its ears. And it can blush with
gorgeous *naïveté* at the thought of making a
social *faux-pas*. It is terribly self-conscious, and
like all growing youth it still has its cosmic
dreams.

Chicago's delight in its Christmas tree is at
the same time the delight of the child in any
glittering gaudily lighted scene, and the delight
of the youth who remembers his baby days and
his passionate belief in Santa Claus and sees in
the great tree a monument to the few years that
have intervened.

There is romance in that thought. Within the
memory of many men and women who walk
beneath the great tree, within the lifetime of
one of the thousands of trees that have been
brought to the making of the great tree and its
lesser relatives, the spot did not exist at all
where now the gigantic realization of a dream of
a Christmas tree stands. It was a wave on its
way to lap a sandy shore, or caught in the
fastnesses of ice. And the shore when it was
reached was a spot where children picnicked in
summer, where horses were brought to the
water's edge for a drink, where wagons were
washed, where the water itself was dipped up in
buckets and carried into the little houses of the
village. It was a spot where bemuffled children
slid back and forth in winter, cautiously keeping
inshore. The spot where the great tree stood the
first time it was made, before the outlying

communities had their separate celebrations, on the land just east of Madison Street and north of the Art Institute, was in the very early days a public burying-ground. Rude storms from the east frequently gnawed at the earth until it had given up its hidden coffins, battered them into fragments, and left scattered, gruesome remains on the shore when the calm came. Within the lifetime of a man it has grown from burying-ground to the waterfront park of one of the great cities of the world.

On any Christmas Eve in those days—and some are still alive who remember it—the smooth motor-filled boulevard which magnificently borders the city was a country road, frozen in deep ruts, or, if the weather had been mild, a sandy morass, thick and impassable. And the streets just west of it, the streets which are filled with Christmas shoppers, with ballyhooers for jumping bunnies and sparklers and little rubber men who stick out their tongues and great tin lobsters which waddle around on the sidewalk, the streets which are thick with human beings and every known mechanical device to lure them and give them comfort and excitement—these same streets were frozen bogs of pathways barely worth the name of road, often with an abandoned cart mutely crying their impassability. Signs proclaiming 'No bottom here' told the tale which the rivers of mud only hinted at. The very street, where an elevated whangs by overhead, a street car clangs its warning to the holiday crowds, and ceaselessly honking motors make a bedlam of the air, is the scene of the classic story of the man who, in the early days, was up to his ears in mud. From a spot identical with one which is being stepped over by thousands, so the story goes, a pedestrian offered to throw out a lifeline to the mud-imprisoned neighbor. 'Don't worry about me,' he is said to have answered, 'I'm on a good horse.' That story delighted our grandfathers.

The sidewalks, lined with gaudy windows wheedling dollars from the passers-by and noisy with street hawkers, passionately supply last-minute gew-gaws for the tired men and women who have had to shop late because they had no money to shop early–sidewalks smooth and wide and sturdy to the tramp of millions of feet–not over a lifetime ago were narrow strips of wood, raised on stilts, with enough room underneath for children to play and for rats to hold continuous convention. Within the memory of its oldest inhabitants those same planks which served as walks were the scene of many a fiasco when an arrogant Indian would calmly push a child off into mud which almost smothered it–an indignity which had to be borne by the members of the community who still remembered the horrors of the Fort Dearborn massacre. Those same lordly concrete ways were the scene in the early days of many a romantic moment when carriages and carts were drawn up to the very doors of the houses and shops and whatever strong male arms that happened to be present were offered to lift the 'wimminfolks' safely from one dry spot to another. High hip boots, they all wore, those early Chicago cavaliers, and of necessity.

Is it not a legitimate glitter of pride in the twinkling eyes of the great tree when it looks upon the vast and teeming loop of the city and remembers that, not so long ago but that men now living can remember, the whole prairie south of the river was a great bog, dry at times, but always at the mercy of every rainfall, and of the seepage from the erratic river that flowed now into the lake and now from it? Ten feet lower than the land to the north of the river it was—this spectacular loop of Chicago, which is unlike the same space of ground anywhere else in the world—and only the dreamers could see that it could ever be made into a city. Is the pride out of place when one remembers that the first civic accomplishment of the village was the gigantic one of raising the level of the south bank and its adjoining acres until it was no longer sick with sogginess? And may it not also be a matter of pride that that river, so gayly going its own unreasoning way, now north, now south, was tamed to the quiet dignity of flowing in one direction?

Would it not give any city a Christmasy feeling of triumph to realize that the land which looks out upon its harbor, land which to-day is weighed in ounces of gold, where great hotels and shops harbor the riches and fripperies of the world, was, within the memory of men and women still actively a part of the city's life, the pasture for the whole town south of the river? It has been many a year since a cow wore down the grass by the roadside of Michigan Avenue, or munched its way about on the prairie, but no more than sixty years ago all of the residents of the South Side took their cows out in the morning and went for them at night. The community practically ended at Wabash and Adams Streets, and the favorite grazing lands were the spots where the Blackstone and Stevens Hotels now have their roots. Even as late as 1871, the year when the world was shocked by the news of the great Chicago fire, cows were still wandering about contentedly in the prairies.

Mayn't the city well wear a mammoth Christmas tree as an adornment this Christmas morning when it looks upon its vastness, when it remembers that, from a mere handful of settlers less than ninety years ago, it has become the home of over three millions? In hundreds of thousands of homes in the vast miles that make Chicago as large and populous as many a monarchy, there are small replicas of the great tree, jeweled with many colored electric bulbs sheltering gifts, each single one of which would have dowered a bride in the older days. A diamond bracelet, dangling to the delight of some eager daughter or wife, is a bauble which, in those days, would have bought the entire loop. A house and an adjacent block of ground could have been purchased with the money that has been spent for one of the many shiny new motor cars that stand in front of hundreds of shiny little brick houses for the first time this Christmas morning.

In the old days, a pair of shoes, woolen underwear, warm mittens, or a highly extravagant 'fascinator' knitted by skillful fingers were the gifts which elicited shrieks of joy from the recipients. An orange was the height of luxury for a child; and he had one orange, not a basket full of them. One wealthy old settler tells with heart-breaking candor of his envy at the sight of a playmate who owned and devoured one large orange before his yearning eyes, and how the memory lasted for years. The highly humanized modern doll, that does everything but think, now walks under the adoring eyes of its 'mama' and says 'Papa' and 'Mama' with equal tenderness to-day. In the early days a little girl was being pampered by her mother when she found among her useful Christmas gifts a creature made of rags and which had to have all of its talking and walking done for it.

Parties all over the city as big as a country are gay with boys and girls home from preparatory schools and colleges and fathers and mothers and grandfathers and grandmothers, all apparently the same age, all living lives made easy by modernity. In the great hotels that face the tree, there are numberless Christmas celebrations, where the guests are all handsomely dinner-jacketed and gowned, all very sophisticated, all having eaten just a little too much and perhaps tippled less wisely than well, dancing something that in the early days of Chicago would have shocked the city fathers. And there is much conversation about the small high-powered roadster that this one found in his Christmas stocking, and the jaunt to Palm Beach as soon as the Christmas gayeties are past, and the new bridge rules, and there is more rich food and bubbly drink. Cosmopolitan, typically modern American they all are, with yearly trips to Europe to furbish up a wardrobe or to buy knick-knacks for the new house. There is as much wealth in the persons of the guests as in the old days the whole territory west of the Hudson would have boasted.

In the memory of one of the grandmothers who is lending, for an hour or so, the dignity of her presence to the party, Christmas was the homiest of the home festivals. The whole season was a simple preparation for the only really passionately anticipated event of the year–New Year's Day. On Christmas there were family gatherings, with long dinners of prairie chicken and whatever frivolities the clever housewife could concoct, with no fresh fruit, no nuts, no out-of-season vegetables, and no skilled French cooks. The 'hired girl' was a blessing (or the curse) of only the few wealthy homes. The caterer had never been heard of, and when he finally did make his appearance fifty or sixty years ago he supplied nothing except ice-cream. In the wealthiest households a fiddler might be had in, but not guests outside the family. Usually, some member of the family had enough talent to play the simple music which the dances required. And such dances! Square, sedate, but hilariously thrilling to grandmother as well as granddaughter.

There would be no extravagantly glittering Christmas trees. Very few families except the Germans had a tree at all. Boughs of evergreen were tacked over the doors and the windows, gathered from the great woods north and west of the city, the woods which are now a part of the most populous miles in Chicago.

If the family happened to live on the north shore of the river and was bid to a family Christmas on the south shore, it dragged itself, of necessity, across the Chicago River on a hand ferry at Rush Street, or crossed at Dearborn Street on a bridge operated by hand cables. And whether the party were joyously gay or not, as moral upright villagers they must needs be at home and in bed by ten o'clock, or, if distance and utter levity demanded, they might possibly sneak in at midnight.

While the tree is still on the lake front, it will watch the mobs rushing into the city on New Year's Eve for the bacchanal which has come to be the American custom of welcoming in the New Year. In the old days, every one was so excited about New Year's Day that they hadn't time to waste on its eve. In the rare households where the ladies of the family were not receiving, a basket was hung on the doorknob in which the callers left their cards. Otherwise, the ladies, furbelowed in their most extravagant gowns, 'received' and kept an accurate account of the number and names of the gentlemen who honored them. The days after New Year's were spent in comparing notes and—for the beaux—in recovering from hot toddy and fried oysters and chicken salad, which the fair hostesses had probably spent half the night before preparing.

The nearest approach to the casual, large, group parties, which the Christmas holidays see nowadays, was, in those days, the Firemen's Ball. Every one who was any one belonged to the fire brigade. The young blades of the village rivaled one another in their devotion to it. A fire was a social event of the first water. The town was very wooden, and fires were frequent and thorough. Whenever one started, the entire town dropped everything and rushed to see the fun. The men dressed themselves up in their *opéra-bouffe* outfits and pumped water–until Long John Wentworth gave them an engine that didn't need hand pumping–and the ladies arrived as soon afterwards as possible with sandwiches and pots of coffee. One met every one at a fire.

It was meet that the Firemen's Ball should be the civic social event of the year. It happened in January. The one in 1847 was a triumph long remembered. There were ten hundred and fifty invitations, all written and delivered by hand (no engravers or post for the meticulous hostesses of those days). It was held in the firehouse and the *élite* of the city attended.

For the Christmas festivities nowadays the long, luxurious trains which roll into Chicago from the East bring many guests who stay a day and dash on to another city in equally luxurious trains. They don't realize it, but the city which they are visiting so casually is the railroad center of the United States. Mankind surges through its land gates as it surges through one of the great ports of the world. But things were far different in the early days. Any one who wanted to be in the village of Chicago for Christmas couldn't decide on December 24th at two o'clock in the afternoon and arrive on Christmas morning from the East. Weeks were spent in the journey. Covered wagons served for the ordinary travelers, but the *élite* came by boat. For a week, if the winds were fair, they were uncomfortable and crowded and badly fed and sick while the boat hurried toward Chicago from Buffalo. And the days they had spent—or weeks—to get to Buffalo! It was never considered much of a trip. They finally arrived and found a town which well deserved its name of 'garden city,' and their enthusiasm for its quiet and comfort after the long hard trip must have had much to do with the increasing numbers which year after year made the arduous trip.

The Christmas feast was not planned the day before Christmas, either. Days of hunting the fowl which were its backbone preceded the work of the housewife. The father and the boys did the shopping for her with guns. There were no great slaughterhouses to supply her with dressed fowl. The packing industry wasn't even heard of. For many years now Chicago has been known as the 'pork-packing town.' Every visitor who comes from overseas insists upon being shown through the 'Yards.' English poets have celebrated Chicago for its stockyards odor, and missed the fresh spiritual fragrance of youth and a zest for life that simply exudes from the city through its smoke and its dirt and its city smells. But in the early days pigs were just pigs, and not a world advertisement. They were a nuisance, not even a luxury. The village had to pass an ordinance that 'any pig or hog running at large without a ring in its nose shall be fined $2.00 collected on conviction of such offense before a justice of peace.' Pigs running around loose in the suavities of Michigan Avenue–isn't that enough to give the giant tree an extra glimmer of mirth and of pride at what the years have done?

In the darkness of the nights between Christmas and New Year's–nights which are now hectic with sirens of motors and the scrape of shifting gears and the continual swish of human voices and the blare of lights–within the memory of men and women living, the quietness of a town safely shut in by its own fireside was in the air, with the occasional call of the town crier–'Lost! Lost! Lost! Little girl seven years old!'

Chicago has left those days behind it, but memories of them make sweeter the complete security and comfort of the city in these days. And the dazzling pyramid of jeweled green, a giant's dream of a Christmas tree, is a symbol of the child's fairy-tale come true. It is a Christmas *boutonnière* tucked into the proud buttonhole of Chicago.

Christmas Crackers

from

Christmas:

Its origin and associations,
Together with
Its historical events and festive
Celebrations during nineteen
Centuries:
Depicting, by pen and pencil,
Memorable celebrations, stately meetings of
early kings,
Remarkable events, romantic episodes, brave
deeds,
Picturesque customs, time-honored sports,
Royal Christmases, coronations and royal
marriages,

Chivalric feats, court banquetings and
revellings,
Christmas at the colleges and the inns of court,
Popular festivities, and Christmas-keeping
In different parts of the world,
Derived from the most authentic
Sources, and arranged
Chronologically.

BY

W. F. DAWSON.

At home, at sea, in many distant lands,

This Kingly Feast without a rival stands!

LONDON

*ELLIOT STOCK, 62, PATERNOSTER ROW,
E.C.*

1902.

CHRISTMAS CRACKERS

One of the popular institutions inseparable from the festivities of Christmastide has long been the "cracker." The satisfaction which young people especially experience in pulling the opposite ends of a gelatine and paper cylinder is of the keenest, accompanied as the operation is by a mixed anticipation—half fearful as to the explosion that is to follow, and wholly delightful with regard to the bonbon or motto which will thus be brought to light. Much amusement is afforded to the lads and lassies by the fortune-telling verses which some of the crackers contain.

A joyous Christmas and happy New Year.

But the cracker of our early days was something far different from what it is now. The sharp "crack" with which the article exploded, and from which it took its name, was then its principal, and, in some cases, its only feature; and the exclamation, "I know I shall scream," which John Leech, in one of his sketches, puts into the mouth of two pretty girls engaged in cracker-pulling, indicated about the all of delight which that occupation afforded.

Since then, however, the cracker has undergone a gradual development. Becoming by degrees a receptacle for bon-bons, rhymed mottoes, little paper caps and aprons, and similar toys, it has passed on to another and higher stage, and is even made a vehicle for high art illustrations. Considerable artistic talent has been introduced in the adornment of these novelties. For instance, the "Silhouette" crackers are illustrated with black figures, comprising portraits of well-known characters in the political, military, and social world, exquisitely executed, while appropriate designs have been adapted to other varieties, respectively designated "Cameos," "Bric-a-brac," "Musical Toys," &c.; and it is quite evident that the education of the young in matters of good taste is not overlooked in the provision of opportunities for merriment.

Letters of Robert E. Lee at Christmas

1862

As published by his son,

in

General Lee, Southern Commander

By Knowledge Keepers Bookstore

"Coosawhatchie, South Carolina, January 18, 1862.

"On my return, day before yesterday, from Florida, dear Mary, I received your letter of the 1st inst. I am very glad to find that you had a pleasant family meeting Christmas, and that it was so large. I am truly grateful for all the mercies we enjoy, notwithstanding the miseries of war, and join heartily in the wish that the next year may find us at peace with all the world.

His friends and admirers were constantly sending him presents; some, simple mementos of their love and affection; others, substantial and material comforts for the outer and inner man. The following letter, from its date, is evidently an acknowledgement of Christmas gifts sent him:

"December 30th (1864).... The Lyons furs and fur robe have also arrived safely, but I can learn nothing of the saddle of mutton. Bryan, of whom I inquired as to its arrival, is greatly alarmed lest it has been sent to the soldiers' dinner. If the soldiers get it, I shall be content. I can do very well without it. In fact, I should rather they should have it than I...."

The soldiers' "dinner" here referred to was a Christmas dinner, sent by the entire country, as far as they could, to the poor starving men in the trenches and camps along the lines. It would not be considered much now, but when the conditions were such as my father describes when he wrote the Secretary of War,

"The struggle now is to keep the army fed and clothed. Only fifty men in some regiments have shoes, and bacon is only issued once in a few days," anything

besides the one-quarter of a pound of bacon and musty corn-bread was a treat of great service, and might be construed as "a Christmas dinner."

"Lexington, Virginia, December 18, 1869.

"My Dear Fitzhugh: I must begin by wishing you a pleasant Christmas and many, many Happy New Years, and may each succeeding year bring to you and yours increasing happiness. I shall think of you and my daughter and my grandson very often during the season when families are generally united, and though absent from you in person, you will always be present in mind, and my poor prayers and best wishes will accompany you all wherever you are.

Christmas in America

From

Christmas:

Its origin and associations,

Together with

Its historical events and festive

Celebrations during nineteen Centuries

By

W. F. Dawson.

1902

Writing just before the Christmas festival of 1855, Mr. Howard Paul says the general manner of celebrating Christmas Day is much the same wherever professors of the Christian faith are found; and the United States, as the great Transatlantic offshoot of Saxon principles, would be the first to conserve the traditional ceremonies handed down from time immemorial by our canonical progenitors of the East. But every nation has its idiocratic notions, minute and otherwise, and it is not strange that the Americans, as a creative people, have peculiar and varied ways of their own in keeping this, the most remarkable day in the calendar. Now and then they add a supplemental form to the accepted code—characteristic of the mutable and progressive spirit of the people—though there still exists the Church service, the conventional carol, the evergreen decorations, the plum-puddings, the pantomime, and a score of other "demonstrations" that never can legitimately be forgotten.

Society generally seems to apportion the day thus: Church in the morning, dinner in the afternoon, and amusements in the evening. The Christmas dinners concentrate the scattered members of families, who meet together to break bread in social harmony, and exchange those home sentiments that cement the happiness of kindred. To-day the prodigal once more returns to the paternal roof; the spendthrift forsakes his boon companions; the convivialist deserts the wine-cup. The beautiful genius of domestic love has triumphed, and who can foresee the blessed results?

Parties, balls, and fêtes, with their endless routine of gaieties, are looked forward to, as pleasures are, the wide world over; and all classes, from highest to lowest, have their modes of enjoyment marked out. Preparation follows preparation in festal succession. Sorrow hides her Gorgon head, care may betake itself to any dreary recesses, for Christmas must be a gala!

There is generally snow on the ground at this time; if Nature is amiable, there is sure to be; and a Christmas sleigh-ride is one of those American delights that defy rivalry. There is no withstanding the merry chime of the bells and a fleet passage over the snow-skirted roads. Town and country look as if they had arisen in the morning in robes of unsullied white. Every housetop is spangled with the bright element; soft flakes are coquetting in the atmosphere, and a pure mantle has been spread on all sides, that fairly invites one to disport upon its gleaming surface.

We abide quietly within our pleasant home on either the eve or night of Christmas. How the sleighs glide by in rapid glee, the music of the bells and the songs of the excursionists falling on our ears in very wildness. We strive in vain to content ourselves. We glance at the cheerful fire, and hearken to the genial voices around us. We philosophize, and struggle against the tokens of merriment without; but the restraint is torture. We, too, must join the revelers, and have a sleigh-ride. Girls, get on your fur; wrap yourselves up warmly in the old bear-skin; hunt up the old guitar; the sleigh is at the door, the moon is beaming. The bells tinkle and away we go!

An old English legend was transplanted many years ago on the shores of America, that took root and flourished with wonderful

luxuriance, considering it was not indigenous to the country. Probably it was taken over to New York by one of the primitive Knickerbockers, or it might have clung to some of the drowsy burgomasters who had forsaken the pictorial tiles of dear old Amsterdam about the time of Peter de Laar, or Il Bombaccia, as the Italians call him, got into disgrace in Rome. However, this may be, certain it is that Santa Claus, or St. Nicholas, the kind Patron-saint of the Juveniles, makes his annual appearance on Christmas Eve, for the purpose of dispensing gifts to all good children. This festive elf is supposed to be a queer little creature that descends the chimney, viewlessly, in the deep hours of night, laden with gifts and presents, which he bestows with no sparing hand, reserving to himself a supernatural discrimination that he seems to exercise with every satisfaction. Before going to bed the children hang their newest stockings near the chimney, or pin them to the curtains of the bed. Midnight finds a world of hosiery waiting for favours; and the only wonder is that a single Santa Claus can get around among them all. The story goes that he never misses one, provided it belongs to a deserving youngster, and morning is sure to bring no reproach that the Christmas Wizard has not nobly performed his wondrous duties. We need scarcely enlighten the reader as to who the real Santa Claus is. Every indulgent parent contributes to the pleasing deception, though the juveniles are strong in their faith of their generous holiday patron. The following favourite lines graphically describe a visit of St. Nicholas, and, being in great vogue with the young people of America, are fondly reproduced from year to year:—

"'Twas the night before Christmas, when all through the house,
Not a creature was stirring, not even a mouse;
The stockings were hung by the chimney with care,

In the hope that St. Nicholas soon would be
there.
The children were nestled all snug in their beds,
While visions of sugar plums danced through
their heads;
And mamma in her 'kerchief, and I in my cap,
Had just settled our brains for a long winter's
nap,
When out on the lawn there arose such a clatter,
I sprang from my bed to see what was the
matter.
The way to the window, I flew like a flash,
Tore open the shutters, and threw up the sash;
The moon on the breast of the new-fallen snow
Gave the lustre of mid-day to objects below.
When what to my wondering eyes should appear
But a miniature sleigh and eight tiny reindeer;
With a little old driver, so lively and quick,
I knew in a moment it must be St. Nick.
More rapid than eagles his coursers they came,
And he whistled, and shouted, and called them
by name—
Now Dasher! now Dancer! Now Prancer! now
Vixen!
On Comet! on Cupid! on Donder and Blixen!
To the top of the porch, to the top of the wall!
Now dash away! dash away! dash away all!'
As the leaves that before the wild hurricane fly,
When they meet with an obstacle, mount to the
sky;
So up to the house-top the coursers they flew,
With the sleigh full of toys, and St. Nicholas too.
And then in a twinkling I heard on the roof,
The prancing and pawing of each little hoof;

As I drew in my head and was turning around,
Down the chimney St. Nicholas came with a
bound.
He was dressed all in furs from his head to his
foot
And his clothes were all tarnished with ashes
and soot.
A bundle of toys he had flung on his back,
And he looked like a pedlar just opening his
pack.
His eyes, how they twinkled! his dimples, how
merry!
His cheeks were like roses, his nose like a
cherry;
His droll little mouth was drawn up like a bow,
And the beard of his chin was as white as the
snow.
The stump of a pipe he held tight in his teeth,
And the smoke it encircled his head like a
wreath.
He had a broad face and a little round belly
That shook when he laughed, like a bowl full of
jelly.
He was chubby and plump—a right jolly old elf;
And I laughed when I saw him, in spite of
myself.
A wink of his eye and a twist of his head
Soon gave me to know I had nothing to dread.
He spoke not a word, but went straight to his
work,
And filled all the stockings—then turned with a
jerk,
And laying his finger aside of his nose,
And giving a nod, up the chimney he rose;

He sprang to his sleigh, to his team gave a
whistle,
And away they all flew like the down of a
thistle.
But I heard him exclaim, ere he drove out of
sight,
'Happy Christmas to all, and to all a good
night!'"

A curious feature of an American Christmas
is the egg-nogg and free lunch, distributed at all
the hotels and cafés. A week at least before the
25th, fanciful signs are suspended over the
fountains of the bars (the hotel-keepers are
quite classic in their ideas) announcing superb
lunch and egg-noggs on Christmas Day. This
invitation is sure to meet with a large response
from the amateur epicures about town, who,
ever on the *qui vive* for a banquet gratis, flock to
the festive standard, since it has never been
found a difficult matter to give things away,
from the time old Heliogabalus gastronomed in
Phœnicia up to the present hour. A splendid
hall in one of the principal hotels, at this
moment, occurs to us. A table, the length of the
apartment, is spread and furnished with twenty
made dishes peculiar to the Christmas *cuisine*.
There
are *chorodens* and *fricassees*, *ragoûts* and *calipee*
, of rapturous delicacy. Each dish is labelled,
and attended by a black servant, who serves its
contents on very small white gilt-edged plates.
At the head of the table a vast bowl,
ornamented with indescribable Chinese figures,
contains the egg-nogg—a palatable compound of

milk, eggs, brandy, and spices, nankeenish in colour, with froth enough on its surface to generate any number of Venuses, if the old Peloponnesian anecdote is worth remembering at all. Over the egg-nogg mine host usually officiates, all smiles and benignity, pouring the rich draught with miraculous dexterity into cut-glass goblets, and passing it to the surrounding guests with profuse hand. On this occasion the long range of fancy drinks are forgotten. Sherry-cobblers, mint-juleps, gin-slings, and punches, are set aside in order that the sway of the Christmas draught may be supreme. Free lunches are extremely common in the United States, what are called "eleven o'clock snacks" especially; but the accompaniment of egg-nogg belongs unequivocally to the death of the year.

The presentation of "boxes" and souvenirs is the same in America as in England, the token of remembrance having an inseparable alliance with the same period. Everybody expects to give and receive. A month before the event the fancy stores are crowded all day long with old and young in search of suitable *souvenirs*, and every object is purchased, from costliest gems to the tawdriest *babiole* that may get into the market. If the weather should be fine, the principal streets are thronged with ladies shopping in sleighs; and hither and thither sleds shoot by, laden with parcels of painted toys, instruments of mock music and septuagenarian dread, from a penny trumpet to a sheepskin drum.

Christmas seems to be a popular period among the young folk for being mated, and a surprising number approach the altar this morning. Whether it is that orange-flowers and bridal gifts are admirably adapted to the time, or that a longer lease of happiness is ensured from the joyous character of the occasion, we are not sufficiently learned in hymeneal lore to announce. The Christmas week, however, is a merry one for the honeymoon, as little is thought of but mirth and gaiety until the dawning New Year soberly suggests that we should put aside our masquerade manners.

In drawing-room amusements society has a wealth of pleasing indoor pastimes. We remember the sententious Question *réunions*, the hilarious Surprise parties, Fairy-bowl, and Hunt-the-slipper[4]. We can never forget the

---

[4] A very popular parlour game, particularly at Victorian family Christmas parties. Oliver Goldsmith's Vicar of Wakefield (1766), chapter 11) provides a lively description: the company at this play plant themselves in a ring upon the ground, all except one, whose business it is to catch a shoe, which the company shove about under their hams from one to another, something like a weaver's shuttle. As it is impossible, in this case, for the lady who is up to face all the company at once, the great beauty of the play lies in hitting her a thump with the heel of the shoe on that side least capable of making a defence.

the company at this play plant themselves in a ring upon the ground, all except one, whose business it is to catch a shoe, which the company shove about under their hams from one to another, something like a weaver's shuttle. As it is impossible, in this case, for the lady who is up to face all the company at once, the great beauty of the play lies vagabond Calathumpians, who employ in their bands everything inharmonious, from a fire-shovel to a stewpan, causing more din than the demons down under the sea ever dreamed of.

What, then, between the sleigh-rides, the bell-melodies, old Santa Claus and his fictions, the egg-nogg and lunches, the weddings and the willingness to be entertained, the Americans find no difficulty in enjoying Christmas Day. Old forms and new notions come in for a share of observances; and the young country, in a glow of good humour, with one voice exclaims, "Le bon temps vienara!"[5]

---

in hitting her a thump with the heel of the shoe on that side least capable of making a defence.

Versions included in Gomme, played by children, involve some play-acting by the seated cobblers pretending to mend shoes and a dialogue between them and the chaser, including a rhyme on the lines of: 'Cobbler, cobbler, mend my shoe, get it done by half-past two'. (Oxford Reference)

[5] Roughly translated "Good times will come."

President Harrison as Santa Claus

1891

Benjamin Harrison was the 23rd
President of the United States from 1889
to 1893

PRESIDENT HARRISON AS "SANTA CLAUS"

Writing from New York on December 22, 1891, a correspondent says: "President Harrison was seen by your correspondent at the White House yesterday, and was asked what he thought about Christmas and its religious and social influences. The President expressed himself willing to offer his opinions, and said: 'Christmas is the most sacred religious festival of the year, and should be an occasion of general rejoicing throughout the land, from the humblest citizen to the highest official, who, for the time being, should forget or put behind him his cares and annoyances, and participate in the spirit of seasonable festivity. We intend to make it a happy day at the White House—all the members of my family, representing four generations, will gather around the big table in the State dining-room to have an old-fashioned Christmas dinner.

Besides Mrs. Harrison, there will be her father, Dr. Scott, Mr. and Mrs. M'Kee and their children, Mrs. Dimmick and Lieutenant and Mrs. Parker. I am an ardent believer in the duty we owe to ourselves as Christians to make merry for children at Christmas time, and we shall have an old-fashioned Christmas tree for the grandchildren upstairs; and I shall be their Santa Claus myself. If my influence goes for aught in this busy world let me hope that my example may be followed in every family in the land.'

"Christmas is made as much of in this country as it is in England, if not more. The plum-pudding is not universal, but the Christmas tree is in almost every home. Even in the tenement districts of the East side, inhabited by the labouring and poorer classes, these vernal emblems of the anniversary are quite as much in demand as in other quarters, and if they and the gifts hung upon them are less elaborate than their West side congeners, the household enthusiasm which welcomes them is quite as marked. As in London, the streets are flooded with Christmas numbers of the periodicals, which, it may be remarked, are this year more elaborate in design and execution than ever. The use of Christmas cards has also obtained surprising proportions. A marked feature of this year's Christmas is the variety and elegance of offerings after the Paris fashion, which are of a purely ornamental and but slight utilitarian character. There are bonbonnières[6] in a variety of forms, some of them very magnificent and expensive; while the Christmas cards range in prices from a cent to ten dollars each. These bonbonnières, decked with expensive ribbon or hand-painted with designs of the season, attain prices as high as forty dollars each, and are in great favour among the wealthy classes. Flowers are also much used, and, just now, are exceedingly costly.

"While the usual religious ceremonies of the day are generally observed here, the mass of the community are inclined to treat the occasion as a festive rather than a solemn occasion, and upon festivity the whole population at the present time seems bent."

---

[6] A box containing trinkets, or "bonbons."

Nebraska Frontier Christmas

As told in

True Stories of Nebraska Pioneers
1880

Published by Knowledge Keepers Bookstore

RANCHING IN GAGE AND JEFFERSON COUNTIES
BY PETER JANSEN

About Christmas, I think it was in 1880, a blizzard started, as they usually did, with a gentle fall of snow, which lasted the first day. During the night, the wind veered to the north, and in the morning, we could not see three rods; it seemed like a sea of milk! We were very anxious to know the fate of our herder and his band of sheep, and towards noon I attempted to reach them, hitching a pair of horses to a sleigh and taking a man along. We soon got lost and drove around in a circle, blinded by the snow, for hours, my companion giving up and resigning himself to death. We probably would have both perished had it not been for the sagacity of my near horse, to which I finally gave the reins, being benummed myself. He brought us home, and you may believe the barking of the shepherd dogs sounded very musical to me as we neared the barn.

A hunter's Christmas dinner

from

*With The World's
Great Travellers*

By

J. S. CAMPION

EDITED BY CHARLES MORRIS
AND OLIVER H. G. LEIGH
Vol. I
CHICAGO

UNION BOOK COMPANY
1901

This story is like so many that American pioneers wrote about: simple celebrations, wild-caught food, and perhaps few or no gifts to exchange. Christmas for Americans has evolved quite dramatically over the centuries!

A HUNTER'S CHRISTMAS DINNER.
J. S. CAMPION.

Campion's "On the Frontier: Reminiscences of Wild Sports, Personal Adventure, and Strange Scenes," a work full of vitality, is the source of our present selection. Some of the author's adventures with hostile Indians are very interesting, but the following account of how the author won his Christmas dinner is likely to prove more attractive reading.

On the evening of December 23 word was brought into camp by one of the hands, who had been looking up the mules, that he had come across the tracks of some twenty-five turkeys, within five or six miles of camp. This was indeed great news. Hope dawned upon us. We should have the fat turkey for Christmas, at all events.

At daylight the next day we started for the spot where the turkey-tracks had been seen; the snow was melted off the low ground, but still lay thick on the cedar and piñon ridges, and in patches on the bottoms.

On arriving at the place we took the trail, and soon ran it to a ridge-top, covered with piñon-trees, on the nuts of which the turkeys had been feeding. Here the tracks spread in all directions, since the turkeys had wandered about, each on his own hook, searching for nuts, and, to double the chances of finding them, we also separated, one going up, the other down the ridge,—going, too, very carefully, for wild turkeys are the most wary of all birds, and require to be hunted with, if possible, more caution than do deer. And we knew not the moment when we might come upon our game, as it was highly probable they were close at hand; for turkeys, if unmolested, daily frequent the same range of feeding-ground, until it is exhausted of food. By and by I came to where eight of the straggling birds had come together and started off again in company. The drove had evidently separated into two or more lots, and I followed the eight turkeys for many miles and for many hours without seeing fresh sign, until at length I came to the edge of a precipitous cliff overlooking a wide part of the valley, the river flowing just below me, and a large grove of big cottonwood-trees in a bottom not far away.

Evidently I was at the place from which the turkeys had flown off the night before to go to roost. I quickly descended, and, going under the cottonwood-trees, searched in the tangle and jungle for sign of their having roosted above, and soon satisfied myself that they had done so. The next step necessary was to discover where the turkeys had alighted in the morning; but this might entail a long search, and, as it was already past noon, I sat down to rest, eat the luncheon I had provided myself with, and come to some conclusion as to which direction I had best choose to make my first cast in.

I had not proceeded far on my way again, when I came suddenly upon a "sign" that arrested my attention and raised hope in my breast,—the tracks of a big fat buck! He had crossed the river-bottom diagonally, and his trail plainly told me all about him: the great width of and the distance between his tracks proclaimed his sex and size, and their depth in the ground his weight. He had been going at an easy trot; the glaze on them was bright, their edges unbroken; not a speck of drifted dust was on them; they were as fresh as new paint. They were not an hour old.

In imagination I smelt roasted venison, and instantly started in pursuit. I followed on the tracks until within an hour of sunset, but never got even a glimpse of the deer; and by that time his trail had brought me to the bank of a stream flowing down one of the side valleys. The buck browsing here and there, but never stopping long in one place, had led me a wide circuit through and over valley and ridges. He had not seen or smelled me, however, since none of his movements showed that he had been alarmed.

The stream, at the place where the deer's track led to it, was unusually wide, consequently slack in current, and therefore frozen over. The snow still lay on the ice, and the buck's track, where he had crossed, looked but just made. The ice seemed firm, and I started to cross the creek. About ten feet from shore, bang through I went, waist deep, into the cold water, and broke and scrambled my way back with great difficulty, and with noise enough to frighten into a gallop any wild animal that might be within a quarter of a mile of me.

It was very disagreeable, very annoying, and *very* cold; and my clothes beginning to freeze on me, I started for camp at a brisk walk.

Just as the sun was going down I passed near to where the turkeys had flown off to roost. It struck me that by watching there a short time I might see them return to the same or a neighboring roost, knowing they often do so. This, however, was very cold work, my clothes being in a half-dried, half-frozen condition; and I was just going to give it up, when I heard the faint distant report of a rifle. The sound redoubled my attention, since I supposed that game was stirring.

In a few minutes I heard the quick sharp alarm call of the turkey, the unmistakable pit-pit, and saw four of them sail off from the edge of the cliff, at about sixty yards' distance from me, into the top branches of the trees forming one of the groups in the valley below. Drawing gently back, and keeping as much as possible under cover, I made my way down into the valley, and started in the direction of the grove of trees in which the turkeys had settled.

It was getting dark, and I had gone but a short way, when, at a distance of about two hundred yards in front, a most extraordinary-looking object presented itself to my view. It looked like a haycock on legs with the handle of a pitchfork sticking out of it; it was steadily advancing through the gloom to where I stood, and arrived quite close to me before I could quite make out what it was. It proved to be my companion, with two turkeys tied together by the legs and slung over his shoulder across his rifle. The wind coming up the valley and blowing the feathers out in all directions had given the turkeys in the gloaming the extraordinary appearance that had astonished me so much. I gave a low whistle, and he joined me; I pointed to the turkeys in the trees. He dropped those he already had, hung them up out of wolf reach, and together we cautiously crept under the four roosting turkeys.

The light was very bad for rifle-shooting, but our front sights were of ivory, and our birds were skyed; so drawing the best beads we could, we fired simultaneously, and with great success, two fine birds dropping dead at our feet,—the others making off.

We congratulated each other, and started for camp with four fat turkeys,—and fat indeed they were, for they had been feeding all autumn on walnuts, hickory-nuts, grapes, sweet acorns, and piñons, at—or rather I suspect without—discretion.

We had a long trudge home, the turkeys getting apparently heavier every mile. As we tramped along my companion related his day's experience. About noon he had come upon the fresh tracks of some turkeys feeding along one of the ridges, and had followed the birds until within about three hours of sunset, when, on peeping into an open glade, he saw fourteen of them scattered over it, picking up seeds and strutting about. As the turkeys seemed to be approaching him, he lay quite still, watching them through the thicket which concealed him. Ultimately they got quite close, giving many fair opportunities to shoot one. But he was determined not to fire unless necessary, preferring to wait for an occasion to present itself enabling him to kill two at one shot,—a very rare chance to obtain. He said it was most interesting to lie there at his ease and watch the motions and movements of the birds as they fed about and spread themselves in fancied security. At last his opportunity came, and firing without a moment's delay, he floored his birds, taking the head of the nearest clean off, and shooting the farther one through the body at the butt of his wings. This was the shot I had heard. I then told him what I had seen, and what had befallen me, and we got home quite done up, but rejoicing at our good luck.

Supper was waiting, and this meal, a blazing fire, and the pipe of peace, recruited us after our fatigues.

We had been very careful and sparing in the use of our spirits, not knowing how long it might be before we should be able to get a fresh supply, or what necessity might arise for their use; but this was considered an occasion when the flowing bowl ought to be indulged in, so grogs all round were mixed and our success celebrated. When this interesting ceremony had been concluded, my companion remarked to me, "Our luck has evidently turned, and, as gamblers always do, we ought to press our good fortune while it lasts. We have got our Christmas turkeys; no doubt the buck you followed is destined to grace our Christmas dinner. I am the man to kill it. Daylight shall see me on his track. You will behold my face no more until I return with the haunches of the big buck." Then he turned in and I quickly followed his example. At the time I had not the remotest idea that my comrade really intended to put his threat into execution; I thought he was "gassing," and put it down to the credit of the flowing bowl.

Next morning I awoke at my usual time,— daybreak,—got out of my blankets, arose, stirred the fire into a great blaze and turned my back to it to get a good warm. I looked for my companion,—his blankets were empty; I glanced towards the arms,—his rifle and belt were gone; I felt his blankets,—they were cold. He had consequently been gone for some time.

I made a cast round, and struck his fresh tracks going in the direction of our last day's tramp. He had "gone for" the big buck. For my part, I was too tired to stir that day. Though then as hard as nails, and in first-rate condition and training, I was thoroughly done up and quite stiff—"played out"—with the previous day's wetting and walking, so remained in camp, and spent the time in helping to make the plum-pudding, dress and stuff the turkeys, and in resting,—principally in resting.

Night came, but not my comrade. I was not exactly uneasy about him, for he was a first-rate hunter and mountaineer; but many are the unexpected accidents that may happen to a lone wanderer in the wilderness.

I piled the wood on the fire and sat waiting for him until near midnight. Then I began to think I was foolish to do so, and had better go to sleep. Just as I was turning in the dogs ran out, frisking and capering, into the darkness. I heard the whistle of my comrade, and he strode into the light of the camp-fire. On his back, in a sling extemporized out of the skin of the deer, were the hind-quarters of a big buck. It was not yet twelve, and though a close shave on being Christmas-day, our bill of fare was filled. Some more flowing bowl.

At breakfast the following day my companion narrated to us the story of his late hunt, as nearly as may be, in the following words:

He said, "By daylight I was where you came to grief by breaking through the ice, with this difference, that I was upon the other side of the creek, having crossed it higher up by means of a beaver dam. Being a cold trail, I pushed ahead sharply, keeping a good lookout, and in a little over two hours came to where the buck had lain down to pass the dark of the night. There being no morning moon, I knew he had not stirred before sunrise, and might, therefore, be browsing, or standing under some tree quite near; so continued my way most cautiously, never following the tracks when they crossed an open, unless obliged to do so on account of the ground being frozen hard, so that it often took me a long time to get his trail again after leaving it; but I knew, if the buck once saw or got a sniff of me, he might run ten miles without stopping.

"About eleven o'clock I sighted him. I was peeping cautiously out of a thicket, at whose edge I had just arrived, into a large park-like glade, and saw him under a big white-oak-tree, eating the acorns. There was no cover between me and where the buck stood, so I could not risk trying to get nearer to him except by making a long detour, and the nearest edge of the timber I was in was too far off him to risk a shot from. There was, therefore, nothing for it but to sit down and wait until he pleased to move on or lie down, and so give me a chance to get nearer. Being hungry, I utilized the time by eating my luncheon, and then fell to smoking. Well, he kept me there over an hour, and then started off in a straight line in a trot. As he took a bee-line for the river, I knew what he was after: he was going to take his 'little drink.' I, too, should have liked to indulge in a little drink, to wash down my luncheon.

"As soon as the buck was well under way I started at the double, on a parallel course, hoping to get a shot at him in the river's bottom. I crossed the open ground of a valley in a bend that was above and out of sight of the course he was taking, got into the cover along the river's bank, and followed it down, but saw nothing of him. By and by I came to where the buck had drunk. He had there crossed the river and gone straight on at a long easy trot towards the Sierra Vérde.

"Should he intend going up the mountain my chance of seeing him again that day was over; if he was going to feed in the piñon ridges, then careful stalking and the avoidance of all mistakes would make him my meat. I could not afford to lose time by going to a beaver dam to cross, so at once peeled and waded over.

"After going about two miles, the buck's tracks showed he had subsided into a walk, and then almost immediately turned, to my great satisfaction, into the piñon-ridge country, in which, after about an hour's careful stalking, I sighted him again. He was strolling along, feeding; but it was getting pretty well on towards sunset before I was able to approach close enough to him to care to fire a shot, for I had taken so much trouble that I was determined to incur no risk I could avoid, but have patience until I had a certainty of killing him in his tracks. At last he stopped to browse in a little open, oval table-land, on the summit of a cedar ridge.

"The ridge-top was nowhere over a hundred yards across, and was surrounded with a thick fringe of dwarf cedars. Peeping through one of these dwarf cedars, I could see the deer's broad fat quarters about forty yards in front of me. The buck was slowly walking from where I stood concealed. I put my cap in a fork of the cedar, laid my rifle-barrel on it, brought its stock to my shoulder, and bleated like a doe.

"The big buck stopped, turned his body half round, his head wholly so, and looked straight towards me with his head down.

"I drew a careful bead between his eyes, and dropped him—stone-dead!

"I ran up to bleed him, feeling quite relieved and glad at so successful a termination of ten hours' difficult hunting. I had not noticed it while engrossed by the interest of pursuit, but now found I was very hungry, and so lit a fire at once, that there might be roasting-coals ready by the time I had skinned my deer.

"I was soon enjoying a jolly rib-roast, making a tremendous meal, and recruiting myself for the tramp of from twelve to fifteen miles lying between me and the camp."

So, after all, we had our Christmas dinner according to programme, and a capital one it was, too.

The turkeys were *à merveille*, the venison delicious; for the big buck—he was nearly as big as a Mexican burro-deer—was very fat indeed. It is only the man who has eaten *really* fat wild venison who knows what good venison *really* is. The kidneys were completely covered with tallow, and my companion assured us that the buck cut nearly an inch of fat on the brisket. The quarters had been hung out to freeze all night, and were thawed in melted snow-water before being cooked, and so were quite tender.

The plum-pudding was over a foot in diameter; we could hardly pull it out of the pot. It was as good as possible, and followed by a bowl of punch, our punch-bowl being for the nonce a tin bucket; not to mince matters, it was our horses' watering-bucket, which, though not elegant, was capacious, and the only utensil we had capable of holding the amount of punch the occasion called for.

No holly grew in the country, but the bright red berries of the Indian arrow-wood and of the bearberry-bush made beautiful substitutes, and there were more evergreens in sight than entire Christendom could have made use of, so our camp was profusely and gaily decorated. Altogether the day was well and duly celebrated, and it is marked with a white stone in the calendar of my memory.

An Engineer's Christmas Story

STORIES *OF THE*
RAILROAD

by

John A. Hill

New York
Doubleday & McClure Co.
1899

AN ENGINEER'S CHRISTMAS STORY

In the summer, fall, and early winter of 1863, I was tossing chips into an old Hinkley insider up in New England, for an engineer by the name of James Dillon. Dillon was considered as good a man as there was on the road: careful, yet fearless, kindhearted, yet impulsive, a man whose friends would fight for him and whose enemies hated him right royally.

Dillon took a great notion to me, and I loved him as a father; the fact of the matter is, he was more of a father to me than I had at home, for my father refused to be comforted when I took to railroading, and I could not see him more than two or three times a year at the most—so when I wanted advice I went to Jim.

I was a young fellow then, and being without a home at either end of the run, was likely to drop into pitfalls. Dillon saw this long before I did. Before I had been with him three months, he told me one day, coming in, that it was against his principles to teach locomotive-running to a young man who was likely to turn out a drunkard or gambler and disgrace the profession, and he added that I had better pack up my duds and come up to his house and let "mother" take care of me—and I went.

I was not a guest there: I paid my room-rent and board just as I should have done anywhere else, but I had all the comforts of a home, and enjoyed a thousand advantages that money could not buy. I told Mrs. Dillon all my troubles, and found kindly sympathy and advice; she encouraged me in all my ambitions, mended my shirts, and went with me when I bought my clothes. Inside of a month, I felt like one of the family, called Mrs. Dillon "mother," and blessed my lucky stars that I had found them.

Dillon had run a good many years, and was heartily tired of it, and he seldom passed a nice farm that he did not call my attention to it, saying: "Jack, now there's comfort; you just wait a couple of years—I've got my eye on the slickest little place, just on the edge of M——, that I am saving up my pile to buy. I'll give you the 'Roger William' one of these days, Jack, say good evening to grief, and me and mother will take comfort. Think of sleeping till eight o'clock,— and no poor steamers, Jack, no poor steamers!" And he would reach over, and give my head a gentle duck as I tried to pitch a curve to a front corner with a knot: those Hinkleys were powerful on cold water.

In Dillon's household there was a "system" of financial management. He always gave his wife just half of what he earned; kept ten dollars for his own expenses during the month, out of which he clothed himself; and put the remainder in the bank. It was before the days of high wages, however, and even with this frugal management, the bank account did not grow rapidly. They owned the house in which they lived, and out of her half "mother" had to pay all the household expenses and taxes, clothe herself and two children, and send the children to school. The oldest, a girl of some sixteen years, was away at normal school, and the boy, about thirteen or fourteen, was at home, going to the public school and wearing out more clothes than all the rest of the family.

Dillon told me that they had agreed on the financial plan followed in the family before their marriage, and he used to say that for the life of him he did not see how "mother" got along so well on the allowance. When he drew a small month's pay he would say to me, as we walked home: "No cream in the coffee this month, Jack." If it was unusually large, he would say: "Plum duff and fried chicken for a Sunday dinner." He insisted that he could detect the rate of his pay in the food, but this was not true—it was his kind of fun. "Mother" and I were fast friends. She became my banker, and when I wanted an extra dollar, I had to ask her for it and tell what I wanted it for, and all that.

Along late in November, Jim had to make an extra one night on another engine, which left me at home alone with "mother" and the boy—I had never seen the girl—and after swearing me to be both deaf, dumb, and blind, "mother" told me a secret. For ten years she had been saving money out of her allowance, until the amount now reached nearly $2,000. She knew of Jim's life ambition to own a farm, and she had the matter in hand, if I would help her. Of course I was head over heels into the scheme at once. She wanted to buy the farm near M———, and give Jim the deed for a Christmas present; and Jim mustn't even suspect.

Jim never did.

The next trip I had to buy some underclothes: would "mother" tell me how to pick out pure wool? Why, bless your heart, no, she wouldn't, but she'd just put on her things and go down with me. Jim smoked and read at home.

We went straight to the bank where Jim kept his money, asked for the President, and let him into the whole plan. Would he take $2,100 out of Jim's money, unbeknown to Jim, and pay the balance of the price of the farm over what "mother" had?

No, he would not; but he would advance the money for the purpose—have the deeds sent to him, and he would pay the price—that was fixed.

Then I hatched up an excuse and changed off with the fireman on the M——— branch, and spent the best part of two lay-overs fixing up things with the owner of the farm and arranging to hold back the recording of the deeds until after Christmas. Every evening there was some part of the project to be talked over, and "mother" and I held many whispered conversations. Once Jim, smiling, observed that, if I had any hair on my face, he would be jealous.

I remember that it was on the 14th day of December, 1863, that payday came. I banked my money with "mother," and Jim, as usual, counted out his half to that dear old financier.

"Uncle Sam'd better put that 'un in the hospital," observed Jim, as he came to a ragged ten-dollar bill. "Goddess of Liberty pretty near got her throat cut there; guess some reb has had hold of her," he continued, as he held up the bill. Then laying it down, he took out his pocket-book and cut off a little three-cornered strip of pink court-plaster, and made repairs on the bill.

"Mother" pocketed her money greedily, and before an hour I had that very bill in my pocket to pay the recording fees in the courthouse at M——.

The next day Jim wanted to use more money than he had in his pocket, and asked me to lend him a dollar. As I opened my wallet to oblige him, that patched bill showed up. Jim put his finger on it, and then turning me around towards him, he said: "How came you by that?"

I turned red—I know I did—but I said, cool enough, "'Mother' gave it to me in change."

"That's a lie," he said, and turned away.

The next day we were more than two-thirds of the way home before he spoke; then, as I straightened up after a fire, he said: "John Alexander, when we get in, you go to Aleck (the foreman) and get changed to some other engine."

There was a queer look on his face; it was not anger, it was not sorrow—it was more like pain. I looked the man straight in the eye, and said: "All right, Jim; it shall be as you say—but, so help me God, I don't know what for. If you will tell me what I have done that is wrong, I will not make the same mistake with the next man I fire for."

He looked away from me, reached over and started the pump, and said: "Don't you know?"

"No, sir, I have not the slightest idea."

"Then you stay, and I'll change," said he, with a determined look, and leaned out of the window, and said no more all the way in.

I did not go home that day. I cleaned the "Roger William" from the top of that mountain of sheet-iron known as a wood-burner stack to the back casting on the tank, and tried to think what I had done wrong, or not done at all, to incur such displeasure[from Dillon. He was in bed when I went to the house that evening, and I did not see him until breakfast. He was in his usual spirits there, but on the way to the station, and all day long, he did not speak to me. He noticed the extra cleaning, and carefully avoided tarnishing any of the cabfittings;—but that awful quiet! I could hardly bear it, and was half sick at the trouble, the cause of which I could not understand. I thought that, if the patched bill had anything to do with it, Christmas morning would clear it up.

Our return trip was the night express, leaving the terminus at 9:30. As usual, that night I got the engine out, oiled, switched out the cars, and took the train to the station, trimmed my signals and headlight, and was all ready for Jim to pull out. Nine o'clock came, and no Jim; at 9:10 I sent to his boarding-house. He had not been there. He did not come at leaving time—he did not come at all. At ten o'clock the conductor sent to the engine-house for another engineer, and at 10:45, instead of an engineer, a fireman came, with orders for John Alexander to run the "Roger William" until further orders,—I never fired a locomotive again.

I went over that road the saddest-hearted man that ever made a maiden trip. I hoped there would be some tidings of Jim at home—there were none. I can never forget the blow it was to "mother;" how she braced up on account of her children—but oh, that sad face! Christmas came, and with it the daughter, and then there were two instead of one: the boy was frantic the first day, and playing marbles the next.

Christmas day there came a letter. It was from Jim—brief and cold enough—but it was such a comfort to "mother." It was directed to Mary J. Dillon, and bore the New York post-mark. It read:

"Uncle Sam is in need of men, and those who lose with Venus may win with Mars. Enclosed papers you will know best what to do with. Be a mother to the children—you have *three* of them.

"JAMES DILLON."

He underscored the three—he was a mystery to me. Poor "mother!" She declared that no doubt "poor James's head was affected." The papers with the letter were a will, leaving her all, and a power of attorney, allowing her to dispose of or use the money in the bank. Not a line of endearment or love for that faithful heart that lived on love, asked only for love, and cared for little else.

That Christmas was a day of fasting and prayer for us. Many letters did we send, many advertisements were printed, but we never got a word from James Dillon, and Uncle Sam's army was too big to hunt in. We were a changed family: quieter and more tender of one another's feelings, but changed.

In the fall of '64 they changed the runs around, and I was booked to run in to M———. Ed, the boy, was firing for me. There was no reason why "mother" should stay in Boston, and we moved out to the little farm. That daughter, who was a second "mother" all over, used to come down to meet us at the station with the horse, and I talked "sweet" to her; yet at a certain point in the sweetness I became dumb.

Along in May, '65, "mother" got a package from Washington. It contained a tintype of herself; a card with a hole in it (made evidently by having been forced over a button), on which was her name and the old address in town; then there was a ring and a saber, and on the blade of the saber was etched, "Presented to Lieutenant Jas. Dillon, for bravery on the field of battle." At the bottom of the parcel was a note in a strange hand, saying simply, "Found on the body of Lieutenant Dillon after the battle of Five Forks."

Poor "mother!" Her heart was wrung again, and again the scalding tears fell. She never told her suffering, and no one ever knew what she bore. Her face was a little sadder and sweeter, her hair a little whiter—that was all.

I am not a bit superstitious—don't believe in signs or presentiments or prenothings—but when I went to get my pay on the 14th day of December, 1866, it gave me a little start to find in it the bill bearing the chromo of the Goddess of

Liberty with the little three-cornered piece of court-plaster that Dillon had put on her windpipe. I got rid of it at once, and said nothing to "mother" about it; but I kept thinking of it and seeing it all the next day and night.

On the night of the 16th, I was oiling around my Black Maria to take out a local leaving our western terminus just after dark, when a tall, slim old gentleman stepped up to me and asked if I was the engineer. I don't suppose I looked like the president: I confessed, and held up my torch, so I could see his face—a pretty tough-looking face. The white mustache was one of that military kind, reinforced with whiskers on the right and left flank of the mustache proper. He wore glasses, and one of the lights was ground glass. The right cheek-bone was crushed in, and a red scar extended across the eye and cheek; the scar looked blue around the red line because of the cold.

"I used to be an engineer before the war," said he. "Do you go to Boston!"

"No, to M——."

"M——! I thought that was on a branch."

"It is, but is now an important manufacturing point, with regular trains from there to each end of the main line."

"When can I get to Boston?"

"Not till Monday now; we run no through Sunday trains. You can go to M—— with me to-night, and catch a local to Boston in the morning."

He thought a minute, and then said, "Well, yes; guess I had better. How is it for a ride?"

"Good; just tell the conductor that I told you to get on."

"Thanks; that's clever. I used to know a soldier who used to run up in this country," said the stranger, musing. "Dillon; that's it, Dillon."

"I knew him well," said I. "I want to hear about him."

"Queer man," said he, and I noticed he was eying me pretty sharp.

"A good engineer."

"Perhaps," said he.

I coaxed the old veteran to ride on the engine— the first coal-burner I had had. He seemed more than glad to comply. Ed was as black as a negro, and swearing about coal-burners in general and this one in particular, and made so much noise with his fire-irons after we started, that the old man came over and sat behind me, so as to be able to talk.

The first time I looked around after getting out of the yard, I noticed his long slim hand on the top of the reverse-lever. Did you ever notice how it seems to make an ex-engineer feel better and more satisfied to get his hand on the reverse-lever and feel the life-throbs of the great giant under him? Why, his hand goes there by instinct—just as an ambulance surgeon will feel for the heart of the boy with a broken leg.

I asked the stranger to "give her a whirl," and noticed with what eager joy he took hold of her. I also observed with surprise that he seemed to know all about "four-mile hill," where most new men got stuck. He caught me looking at his face, and touching the scar, remarked: "A little love pat, with the compliments of Wade Hampton's men." We talked on a good many subjects, and got pretty well acquainted before we were over the division, but at last we seemed talked out.

"Where does Dillon's folks live now?" asked the stranger, slowly, after a time.

"M——," said I.

He nearly jumped off the box. "M——? I thought it was Boston!"

"Moved to M——."

"What for?"

"Own a farm there."

"Oh, I see; married again?"

"No."

"No!"

"Widow thought too much of Jim for that."

"No!"

"Yes."

"Er—what became of the young man that they—er—adopted?"

"Lives with 'em yet."

"So!"

Just then we struck the suburbs of M——, and, as we passed the cemetery, I pointed to a high shaft, and said: "Dillon's monument."

"Why, how's that?"

"Killed at Five Forks. Widow put up monument."

He shaded his eyes with his hand, and peered through the moonlight for a minute.

"That's clever," was all he said.

I insisted that he go home with me. Ed took the Black Maria to the house, and we took the street cars for it to the end of the line, and then walked. As we cleaned our feet at the door, I said: "Let me see, I did not hear your name?"

"James," said he, "Mr. James."

I opened the sitting-room door, and ushered the stranger in.

"Well, boys," said "mother," slowly getting up from before the fire and hurriedly taking a few extra stitches in her knitting before laying it down to look up at us, "you're early."

She looked up, not ten feet from the stranger, as he took off his slouched hat and brushed back the white hair. In another[Pg 24] minute her arms were around his neck, and she was murmuring "James" in his ear, and I, like a dumb fool, wondered who told her his name.

Well, to make a long story short, it was James Dillon himself, and the daughter came in, and Ed came, and between the three they nearly smothered the old fellow.

You may think it funny he didn't know me, but don't forget that I had been running for three years—that takes the fresh off a fellow; then, when I had the typhoid, my hair laid off, and was never reinstated, and when I got well, the whiskers—that had always refused to grow— came on with a rush, and they were red. And again, I had tried to switch with an old hook-motion in the night and forgot to take out the starting-bar, and she threw it at me, knocking out some teeth; and taking it altogether, I was a changed man.

"Where's John?" he said finally.

"Here," said I.

"No!"

"Yes."

He took my hand, and said, "John, I left all that was dear to me once, because I was jealous of you. I never knew how you came to have that money or why, and don't want to. Forgive me."

"That is the first time I ever heard of that," said "mother."

"I had it to buy this farm for you—a Christmas present—if you had waited," said I.

"That is the first time I ever heard of that," said he.

"And you might have been shot," said "mother," getting up close.

"I tried my darndest to be. That's why I got promoted so fast."

"Oh, James!" and her arms were around his neck again.

"And I sent that saber home myself, never intending to come back."

"Oh, James, how could you!"

"Mother, how can you forgive me?"

"Mother," was still for a minute, looking at the fire in the grate. "James, it is late in life to apply such tests, but love is like gold; ours will be better now—the dross has been burned away in the fire. I did what I did for love of you, and you did what you did for love of me; let us all commence to live again in the old way," and those arms of hers could not keep away from his neck.

Ed went out with tears in his eyes, and I beckoned the daughter to follow me. We passed into the parlor, drew the curtain over the doorway—and there was nothing but that rag between us and heaven.

Origin of the Christmas Card

from

The Book of Christmas

New York
The Macmillan
Company
1909

Origin of the Christmas Card

W. S. WALSH in *Curiosities of Popular Customs*

THE Christmas Card is the legitimate descendant of the "school pieces" or "Christmas pieces" which were popular from the beginning to the middle of the nineteenth century. These were sheets of writing-paper sometimes surrounded with those hideous and elaborate pen flourishes forming birds, scrolls, etc., so unnaturally dear to the hearts of writing masters, and sometimes headed with copper-plate engravings, plain or colored. These were used by school boys at the approach of holidays for carefully written letters exploiting the progress they had made in composition and chirography. Charity boys were large purchasers of these pieces, says one writer, and at Christmas time used to take them round their parish to show and at the same time solicit a trifle.

The Christmas Card proper had its tentative origin in 1846. Mr. Joseph Cundall, a London artist, claims to have issued the first in that year. It was printed in lithography, colored by hand, and was of the usual size of a lady's card.

Not until 1862, however, did the custom obtain any foothold. Then experiments were made with cards of the size of an ordinary *carte de visite*, inscribed simply "A Merry Christmas" and "A Happy New Year." After that came to be added robins and holly branches, embossed[Pg 68] figures and landscapes. "I have the original designs before me now," wrote "Luke Limner" (John Leighton) to the London *Publishers' Circular*, Dec. 31, 1883: "they were produced by Goodall & Son. Seeing a growing want and the great sale obtained abroad, this house produced (1868) a Little Red Riding Hood, a Hermit and his Cell, and many other subjects in which snow and the robin played a part."

The Yule Clog

T. K. HERVEY

from

The Book of Christmas

New York
The Macmillan
Company
1909

The Yule Clog

T. K. HERVEY

AMID the interior forms to be observed, on this evening, by those who would keep their Christmas after the old orthodox fashion, the first to be noticed is that of the Yule Clog[7]. This huge block, which, in ancient times, and consistently with the capacity of its vast receptacle, was frequently the root of a large tree, it was the practice to introduce into the house with great ceremony, and to the sound of music.

In Drake's "Winter Nights" mention is made of the Yule Clog, as "lying, in ponderous majesty, on the kitchen floor," until "each had sung his Yule song, standing on its centre,"—ere it was consigned to the flames that

"Went roaring up the chimney wide."

This Yule Clog, according to Herrick, was to be lighted with the brand of the last year's log, which had been carefully laid aside for the purpose, and music was to be played during the ceremony of lighting.

---

[7] It was commonly called a "Yule Clog" in north-east England.

This log appears to have been considered as sanctifying the roof-tree, and was probably deemed a protection against those evil spirits over whom this season was in every way a triumph. Accordingly, various superstitions mingled with the prescribed ceremonials in respect of it. From the authority already quoted on this subject, we learn that its virtues were not to be extracted unless it were lighted with clean hands—a direction, probably, including both a useful household hint to the domestics, and, it may be, a moral of a higher kind:—

> *"Wash your hands or else the fire*
> *Will not tend to your desire;*
> *Unwash'd hands, ye maidens, know,*
> *Dead the fire though ye blow."*

Around this fire, when duly lighted, the hospitalities of the evening were dispensed; and as the flames played about it and above it, with a pleasant song of their own, the song and the tale and the jest went cheerily round.

Merry Christmas in the Tenements

BY JACOB RIIS in *Children of the Tenements*

from

The Book of Christmas

New York
The Macmillan
Company
1909

Merry Christmas in the Tenements

BY JACOB RIIS in *Children of the Tenements*

IT was just a sprig of holly, with scarlet berries showing against the green, stuck in, by one of the office boys probably, behind the sign that pointed the way up to the editorial rooms. There was no reason why it should have made me start when I came suddenly upon it at the turn of the stairs; but it did. Perhaps it was because that dingy hall, given over to dust and draughts all the days of the year, was the last place in which I expected to meet with any sign of Christmas; perhaps it was because I myself had nearly forgotten the holiday. Whatever the cause, it gave me quite a turn.

I stood, and stared at it. It looked dry, almost withered. Probably it had come a long way. Not much holly grows about Printing-House Square, except in the colored supplements, and that is scarcely of a kind to stir tender memories. Withered and dry, this did. I thought, with a twinge of conscience, of secret little conclaves of my children, of private views of things hidden from mamma at the bottom of drawers, of wild flights when papa appeared unbidden in the door, which I had allowed for once to pass unheeded. Absorbed in the business of the office, I had hardly thought of Christmas coming on, until now it was here. And this sprig of holly on the wall that had come to remind me,—come nobody knew how far,—did it grow yet in the beechwood clearings, as it did when I gathered it as a boy, tracking through the snow? "Christ-thorn" we called it in our Danish tongue. The red berries, to our simple faith, were the drops of blood that fell from the Saviour's brow as it dropped under its cruel crown upon the cross....

* * * * * * *

The lights of the Bowery glow like a myriad twinkling stars upon the ceaseless flood of humanity that surges ever through the great highway of the homeless. They shine upon long rows of lodging-houses, in which hundreds of young men, cast helpless upon the reef of the strange city, are learning their first lessons of utter loneliness; for what desolation is there like that of the careless crowd when all the world rejoices? They shine upon the tempter setting his snares there, and upon the missionary and the Salvation Army lass, disputing his catch with him; upon the police detective going his rounds with coldly observant eye intent upon the outcome of the contest; upon the wreck that is past hope, and upon the youth pausing on the verge of the pit in which the other has long ceased to struggle. Sights and sounds of Christmas there are in plenty in the Bowery. Balsam and hemlock and fir stand in groves along the busy thoroughfare, and garlands of green embower mission and dive impartially. Once a year the old street recalls its youth with an effort. It is true that it is largely a commercial effort; that the evergreen, with an instinct that is not of its native hills, haunts saloon-corners by preference; but the smell of the pine woods is in the air, and—Christmas is not too critical—one is grateful for the effort. It varies with the opportunity. At "Beefsteak John's" it is content with artistically embalming crullers and mince-pies in green cabbage under the window lamp. Over yonder, where the mile-post of the old lane still stands,—in its unhonored old age become the vehicle of publishing the latest "sure cure" to the world,—a florist, whose undenominational zeal for the holiday and trade outstrips alike distinction of creed and property, has transformed the sidewalk and the ugly railroad structure into a veritable bower, spanning it with a canopy of green, under which dwell with him, in neighborly good-will, the Young Men's Christian Association and the Jewish tailor next door....

Down at the foot of the Bowery is the "panhandlers' beat," where the saloons elbow one another at every step, crowding out all other business than that of keeping lodgers to support them. Within call of it, across the square, stands a church which, in the memory of men yet living, was built to shelter the fashionable Baptist audiences of a day when Madison Square was out in the fields, and Harlem had a foreign sound. The fashionable audiences are gone long since.

To-day the church, fallen into premature decay, but still handsome in its strong and noble lines, stands as a missionary outpost in the land of the enemy, its builders would have said, doing a greater work than they planned. To-night is the Christmas festival of its English-speaking Sunday-school, and the pews are filled. The banners of United Italy, of modern Hellas, of France and Germany and England, hang side by side with the Chinese dragon and the starry flag-signs of the cosmopolitan character of the congregation. Greek and Roman Catholics, Jews and joss-worshippers, go there; few Protestants, and no Baptists. It is easy to pick out the children in their seats by nationality, and as easy to read the story of poverty and suffering that stands written in more than one mother's haggard face, now beaming with pleasure at the little ones' glee. A gayly decorated Christmas tree has taken the place of the pulpit. At its foot is stacked a mountain of bundles, Santa Claus's gifts to the school. A self-conscious young man with soap-locks had just been allowed to retire, amid tumultuous applause, after blowing "Nearer, my God, to Thee" on his horn until his cheeks swelled almost to bursting. A trumpet ever takes the Fourth Ward by storm. A class of little girls is climbing upon the platform. Each wears a capital letter on her breast, and together they spell its lesson. There is momentary consternation: one is missing. As the discovery is made, a child pushes past the doorkeeper, hot and breathless. "I am in

'Boundless Love,'" she says, and makes for the platform, where her arrival restores confidence and the language.

In the audience the befrocked visitor from up-town sits cheek by jowl with the pigtailed Chinaman and the dark-browed Italian. Up in the gallery, farthest from the preacher's desk and the tree, sits a Jewish mother with three boys, almost in rags. A dingy and threadbare shawl partly hides her poor calico wrap and patched apron. The woman shrinks in the pew, fearful of being seen; her boys stand upon the benches, and applaud with the rest. She endeavors vainly to restrain them. "Tick, tick!" goes the old clock over the door through which wealth and fashion went out long years ago, and poverty came in....

Within hail of the Sullivan Street school camps a scattered little band, the Christmas customs of which I had been trying for years to surprise. They are Indians, a handful of Mohawks and Iroquois, whom some ill wind has blown down from their Canadian reservation, and left in these West Side tenements to eke out such a living as they can, weaving mats and baskets, and threading glass pearls on slippers and pin-cushions, until one after another they have died off and gone to happier hunting-grounds than Thompson Street. There were as many families as one could count on the fingers of both hands when I first came upon them, at the death of old Tamenund, the basket maker. Last Christmas there were seven. I had about made up my mind that the only real Americans in New York did not keep the holiday at all, when one Christmas eve they showed me how. Just as dark was setting in, old Mrs. Benoit came from her Hudson Street attic—where she was known among the neighbors, as old and poor as she, as Mrs. Ben Wah, and was believed to be the relict of a warrior of the name of Benjamin Wah—to the office of the Charity Organization Society, with a bundle for a friend who had helped her over a rough spot—the rent, I suppose. The bundle was done up elaborately in blue cheese-cloth, and contained a lot of little garments which she had made out of the remnants of blankets and cloth of her own from a younger and better day. "For those," she said, in her French patois, "who are poorer than myself;" and hobbled away. I found out, a few days later, when I took her picture weaving mats in the attic room, that she had scarcely food in the house that Christmas day and not the car fare to take her to church! Walking was bad, and her old limbs were stiff. She sat by the window through the winter evening and watched the sun go down behind the western hills, comforted by her pipe. Mrs. Ben Wah, to give her her local name, is not really an Indian; but her husband was one, and she lived all her life with the tribe till she came here. She is a philosopher in her own quaint way. "It is no disgrace to be poor," said she to me, regarding her empty tobacco-pouch; "but it is sometimes a great inconvenience." Not even the recollection of the vote of censure that was passed upon me once by the ladies of the Charitable Ten for surreptitiously supplying an aged couple, the special object of their charity, with army plug, could have deterred me from taking the hint....

In a hundred places all over the city, when Christmas comes, as many open-air fairs spring suddenly into life. A kind of Gentile Feast of Tabernacles possesses the tenement districts especially. Green-embowered booths stand in rows at the curb, and the voice of the tin trumpet is heard in the land. The common source of all the show is down by the North River, in the district known as "the Farm." Down there Santa Claus establishes headquarters early in December and until past New Year. The broad quay looks then more like a clearing in a pine forest than a busy section of the metropolis. The steamers discharge their loads of fir trees at the piers until they stand stacked mountain high, with foot-hills of holly and ground-ivy trailing off toward the land side. An army train of wagons is engaged in carting them away from early morning till late at night; but the green forest grows, in spite of it all, until in places it shuts the shipping out of sight altogether. The air is redolent with the smell of balsam and pine. After nightfall, when the lights are burning in the busy market, and the homeward-bound crowds with baskets and heavy burdens of Christmas greens jostle one another with good-natured banter,—nobody is ever cross down here in the holiday season,—it is good to take a stroll through the Farm, if one has a spot in his heart faithful yet to the hills and the woods in spite of the latter-day city. But it is when the moonlight is upon the water and upon the dark phantom forest, when the heavy breathing of some passing steamer is the only sound that breaks the stillness of the night, and the watchman smokes his only pipe on the bulwark, that the Farm has a mood and an atmosphere all its own, full of poetry which some day a painter's brush will catch and hold....

Farthest down town, where the island narrows toward the Battery, and warehouses crowd the few remaining tenements, the sombre-hued colony of Syrians is astir with preparation for the holiday. How comes it that in the only settlement of the real Christmas people in New York the corner saloon appropriates to itself all the outward signs of it? Even the floral cross that is nailed over the door of the Orthodox church is long withered and dead; it has been there since Easter, and it is yet twelve days to Christmas by the belated reckoning of the Greek Church. But if the houses show no sign of the holiday, within there is nothing lacking. The whole colony is gone a-visiting. There are enough of the unorthodox to set the fashion, and the rest follow the custom of the country. The men go from house to house, laugh, shake hands, and kiss one another on both cheeks, with the salutation, "Kol am va antom Salimoon. " "Every year and you are safe," the Syrian guide renders it into English; and a non-professional interpreter amends it: "May you grow happier year by year." Arrack made from grapes and flavored with aniseseed, and candy baked in little white balls like marbles, are served with the indispensable cigarette; for long callers, the pipe....

The bells in old Trinity chime the midnight hour. From dark hallways men and women pour forth and hasten to the Maronite church. In the loft of the dingy old warehouse wax candles burn before an altar of brass. The priest, in a white robe with a huge gold cross worked on the back, chants the ritual. The people respond. The women kneel in the aisles, shrouding their heads in their shawls; a surpliced acolyte swings his censer; the heavy perfume of burning incense fills the hall.

The band at the anarchists' ball is tuning up for the last dance. Young and old float to the happy strains, forgetting injustice, oppression, hatred. Children slide upon the waxed floor, weaving fearlessly in and out between couples—between fierce, bearded men and short-haired women with crimson-bordered kerchiefs. A Punch-and-Judy show in the corner evokes shouts of laughter.

Outside the snow is falling. It sifts silently into each nook and corner, softens all the hard and ugly lines, and throws the spotless mantle of

charity over the blemishes, the shortcomings.
Christmas morning will dawn pure and white.

Christmas Dinner
&
Christmas Cheer

COMMON-SENSE PAPERS ON
COOKERY

BY

A G PAYNE

CASSELL PETTER & GALPIN:
London, Paris & New York.

1880

CHRISTMAS DINNER

Once more the season has come round in which our Saviour's birth is celebrated, and though more than eighteen centuries have passed away, still the clarion voice rings as fresh as ever in our ears—"Goodwill toward men." From the highest to the lowest the sacred charm still works its magic spell. What child was ever sent to bed before its time, no matter what the crime, on Christmas Day? Oh, if we could only embed in our hearts throughout the year one half the charity that for very shame seems forced on us on this great festival, how far happier should we be!

It is not, however, now my province to dwell upon the sacred character of the day, yet the whole subject is so deep, so unfathomable, that, like a still phosphorescent sea, the slightest touch is instantly surrounded by a halo of glory, faintly and dimly revealing to finite minds the infinite brightness that is hidden in its breast, and I cannot bear to enter into the practical details of the day's festivities without some slight allusion in honour of the Author and Founder of the feast.

Now—the higher duties of the season being of course left out of the question—Christmas Day without its dinner would be like the play of

"Hamlet" with the part of Hamlet omitted. A genuine Christmas dinner, too, reveals our real national taste, and proves to ourselves and all the world that we have not yet acquired a French one. I wonder if it is possible for a statistician to calculate how many huge sirloins of beef and immense turkeys are consumed on Christmas Day. Such substantial fare—so unkickshawlike. Nor must we forget the goose of humbler life. Were it possible to calculate the exact amount of gratification given by mere eating, it would probably be found that the aristocratic sirloin and turkey fail to compare with the goose and sage and onion. We may add, especially the sage and onion.

We will suppose the happy morning to have arrived, and the children gathered round the table, with cheeks so flushed with pleasure and anticipation that they rival in colour the bright-red berries that glisten in the holly on the walls. Bright eyes to match the bright cheeks, eyes that have sparkled brighter as the well-known and looked-for chink has occurred, as the annual Christmas-box has been slipped into the hand by the grey-haired father or uncle, as the case may be—whose own eye is tinged with water as his mind goes back to the time, too, when he himself was a boy, without a care or thought of the morrow, and who, conscious of the joy he's giving, walks away with a lighter pocket but far lighter heart.

Happy, happy times! Is there one who at such a moment has an anxious care? Yes—suppose the beef should be raw, the mince-pie burnt, and the pudding all tumble to pieces the moment it is turned out. Were it known, I daresay tears have been shed upon such trifles; but then trifles make up life.

Perhaps the deepest anxiety is about the pudding. I will give the following recipe, which I have always found an excellent one. The ingredients required are—one pound and a half of muscatel raisins, half a pound of currants, quarter of a pound of sultana raisins, half a pound of mixed candied peel, three-quarters of a pound of bread-crumbs, three-quarters of a pound of suet chopped fine, nine eggs, quarter of an ounce of pounded bitter almonds, a table-spoonful of flour, a table-spoonful of moist sugar, and a quarter of a pint of brandy.

The first thing to do is to stone the raisins. Cut the raisins into two pieces, and in taking out the pips or stones be careful not to take out the pulp. For this reason it is undesirable to leave the stoning of the raisins to young persons. It is more than human nature can bear, and the strongest-minded child is apt to suck his or her fingers during the process, which, in addition to being far from nice, is apt to detract from the rich muscatel flavour of the pudding. The currants should be bought some days before they are wanted, in order that they may be first washed and then dried. Spread them out on a large sheet of coarse paper before the kitchen fire, and occasionally stir them about. They will also require picking, and this wants both care and patience; those little tiny stalks of the currants are very disagreeable to get into the mouth, and still more into a hollow tooth, for which they seem to have a natural affinity. The candied peel should be sliced into little, very thin slices, and not chopped up. The bread-crumbs should be made as fine as possible, and the suet chopped up very fine. Care should be taken to get the very best beef suet, that will chop properly, as some suet has a tendency to get into a creamy mass; when this is the case it is impossible to make a proper pudding of it. The dry ingredients should now be placed in a large basin, and thoroughly mixed together, care being taken to put in the pounded bitter almonds little by little. The eggs should be broken one by one into a cup, in order to see that each one is perfectly fresh. One stale egg will quite spoil a pudding. Beat up the eggs all together till they froth, and mix them in with the rest, and add the brandy. If the bread-crumbs were properly dried, it would not be found to be too moist.

Next take a new pudding-cloth, that has been well boiled in plain water, and butter it thoroughly, and then flour it. Turn the pudding into it and tie it, leaving room for the pudding to swell. The cloth must be fastened very securely, and it is as well to tie it in two places, in case of accidents. This pudding must now be boiled for at least six hours. It will always be found best to make the pudding some days before it is required; hang it up in the cloth, putting something underneath it to catch the drops; and a pudding made as we have directed will keep good for months and months. It only requires warming up for a couple of hours in a large saucepan of boiling water, and then turning out.

Now that awfully critical moment—turning out. Care should be taken to peel off the cloth, and not pull it; the reason of this is self-evident. On Christmas Day a piece of bright holly, with some red berries on it, should be stuck on the top of the pudding, and some lighted brandy poured over and round it. If you take my advice, you will light the brandy in the room.

To carry a large flat dish with ignited brandy is extremely dangerous, and I have not forgotten that dreadful story which appeared in the papers one or two years ago, about the poor girl who was burnt to death by the lighted brandy from the Christmas pudding falling on her white muslin dress.

In order to light the brandy, get a large iron spoon and fill it with brandy, get a lighted cedar taper or thin wood-shaving, or even a piece of paper rolled up, and act exactly as if you were going to boil the brandy in the spoon; in a few minutes the brandy will light of its own accord, when it can be poured on the pudding, and more added if required. If it is evening, and young children are present, it is as well to turn down the gas very low, or remove the candle for a few minutes. Judging by my own recollections, the lighted plum pudding was a great event in my early days—slightly awful, but intensely delightful.

With regard to the beef, I need say but a few words. It is a question between you and the butcher, and I will say butchers, as a rule, behave very well at Christmas-time, and while I think of it, I would recommend you to give your carving-knife to the butcher-boy, and tell him to get it well sharpened for the occasion, a hint that will not be forgotten—the day after Christmas will have its due effect. But sirloin of beef has a trying piece of gristle at the top, and without a sharp knife a very handsome piece will be made to look ragged. Have a good roaring fire. A piece about twelve pounds will take three hours. It will not require much basting, but remind the cook that it is the sides, and not the fat part, that should be basted. Some stupid women forget this. Let the dish for the beef be thoroughly hot; and this takes time. Have also some curly white horseradish to pile on the top of the joint, and be sure the dish-cover is hot, without being smoking.

We will next discuss the mincemeat, and would recommend a trial of the following recipe:—Take three apples, three lemons, one pound of raisins, three-quarters of a pound of currants, one pound of suet, quarter of a pound of raw beef, two pounds of moist sugar, four ounces of mixed candied peel, quarter of a rind of a fresh orange, one tea-spoonful of powdered mixed spice composed of equal proportions of cloves, cinnamon, and nutmeg; half a pint of brandy, and one glass of port wine.

Peel the apples and cut out the cores very carefully, and then bake the pieces till they are quite soft. Squeeze the lemons, and cut away the white pappy part, and boil the lemon-peel till it is fairly soft. The raisins must of course be carefully stoned, and the currants well washed and dried, and picked, as in the case of the pudding. Chop the suet very finely, as well as the raw meat and lemon-peel. Mix all the ingredients well together, and add the brandy last of all, and press the whole down into a stone jar, and place a piece of paper soaked in brandy on the top. Remove the paper and stir up the mixture thoroughly every three days, replacing the paper; if this is done, the mincemeat will keep good a long time.

To make the pies, roll out some thin puff-paste, butter a small round tin, and line it with a piece of paste, then place in a generous quantity of the mincemeat, and cover it over with a similar piece of puff-paste, and bake it in a moderate oven. Mince pies are none the worse for being warmed up, but pray take care that they are sent to table hot.

Let us next proceed to the goose. Now a fine, large, tender goose, with a sauce-tureen of fine rich gravy, and another of hot apple sauce, with a nice large floury potato, is not to be despised, and to my mind is worth half a dozen turkeys. I am afraid the sage and onion, the necessary accompaniment, causes it to be considered rather a vulgar dish. Never mind, let us be vulgar; it's only once a year. The principal thing is the stuffing. Onions vary so in size that it is a little difficult to describe, but for a large goose you must take five large onions and ten fresh sage-leaves. If you are obliged to put up with dried leaves, you will want nearly twice the number. Take rather more than a quarter of a pound of bread-crumbs, about a couple of ounces of butter, and add some black pepper and salt.

Chop the onions very fine with the sage-leaves, and mix all up together; and the yolks of a couple of eggs may be added if you wish to have the seasoning very rich, but they are by no means necessary.

This will make the stuffing that nine persons out of ten really prefer, but do not like to say so. If, therefore, you really wish to have the stuffing mild, the only difference must be, you must cut out the cores of the onions and partially boil them, and let them drain on a napkin; this takes away considerably the strong onion-flavour of which some persons are not very fond. Fill the goose with the stuffing, and roast it before a quick fire. Care must be taken that the goose is well tied up, to prevent the stuffing coming out at one end, or its getting filled with grease during basting at the other. A good-sized goose only requires one hour and a half to roast, and the general fault is that people will over-roast them, and dry them up. The largest goose I have ever seen would not take more than two hours, but try in the case of a very large one to have the stuffing off the chill before you put it in. Serve some rich brown gravy and apple sauce in a separate tureen, as you will be sure to splash the gravy in carving the goose if any is put on the dish.

With regard to roast turkey I can only say that no possible time can be given for roasting, as they vary so—especially in the present day of plump prize birds—that even the weight would be no criterion. A small turkey will require one hour and a half; while a very large one may want five hours. One word of caution about the stuffing. Every one knows how unpleasant a tendency what is called veal stuffing has to "rise." This is, I believe, owing to too much lemon-peel being almost invariably used. When you use a quarter of a pound of beef suet, a quarter of a lemon is amply sufficient. To this quantity may be added a couple of tea-spoonfuls of dried mixed stuffing-herbs (which can be bought in bottles at Covent Garden Market), two ounces of lean ham, rather more than a quarter of a pound of bread-crumbs, two eggs, a little chopped parsley (about a tea-spoonful or rather more), and a little grated nutmeg, salt, and cayenne pepper. Mince all the ingredients very finely together, and pound them afterwards in a mortar.

A very nice stuffing for turkeys can be made from chestnuts, but space will not allow me to enter into further details.

In conclusion, let me add, let Christmas come as a blessing, and not as a curse.

The demon Alcohol is abroad at this holy season, and many know that they require an archangel's strength to trample him underfoot. Let the law of each feast be regulated like that of the wise Eastern monarch: "None did compel." Let every one on Christmas Eve endeavour to find some case of distress which it is real and not false charity to alleviate. He will doubly enjoy his own dinner who can think that some one but for him would have gone without. It is such deeds that entitle us to say—

—— —— —— ——"That his bones,
When he has run his course, and sleeps in blessings,
May have a tomb of orphans' tears wept on 'em."

CHRISTMAS CHEER

There is something sacred in the very name of *home* to every true-born Englishman, and, as we should naturally expect from the hallowing influence of this holy season of the year, home seems doubly sacred on Christmas Day. How many thousand families throughout the land are united but once a year! what efforts, too, do some make, so that on their great annual holiday they may once again find shelter under the old and loving parental wings!

But let us this year anticipate the day's festivities, and Christmas Eve finds us once again reunited round the fire, on which the log is heaped, and crackles brightly: for no one, unless by abject poverty compelled, would have a poor fire on Christmas Eve. The fresh-cut holly glistens on the wall, the curtains are drawn, and the grey-haired, bright-eyed old man, as he glances round the circle, his voice too full almost to speak, yet feels an inner comfort difficult to describe—a feeling partly of thankfulness, partly of resignation, as he looks forward to the fast-approaching time when the places that know him now shall know him no more for ever. For it has been well said that children, though they increase the cares of life, yet mitigate the remembrance of death. But such a good old-fashioned circle round the fire on such a night would not be complete without a steaming bowl of something hot, to drink a toast in memory of yet another happy gathering in the old house at home. So, while the party assembled listen to the distant sound of the waits, or perhaps to the still preferable music of the bird of dawn—which recalls one of the brightest gems that have dropped from the pen of our greatest poet—we will, after repeating the lines, step down-stairs, and brew a bowl of bishop:—

> "Some say that ever, that season comes
> Wherein our Saviour's birth is celebrated,
> This bird of dawning singeth all night long:
> And then, they say, no spirit dares stir abroad:
> The nights are wholesome; then no planets strike,
> No fairy takes, nor witch hath power to charm,
> So hallowed and so gracious is the time."

Bishop, a good old-fashioned drink, whose nose has, so to speak, been somewhat put out of joint by mulled claret since that beverage has become so cheap, is best made as follows:—First take a small lemon, and at this season of the year they will be easily obtained white and new. First wash the lemon in a little warm water, and then stick into it a dozen or more cloves, and make the lemon hot by placing it in a plate in the oven, or better still, by suspending it from a string in front of the fire, taking care that the lemon does not hang too close, so as to get so hot as to split. Next take a little water, about a tumblerful, and pour it into an enamelled saucepan, and add to it a stick of cinnamon about six inches long—of course, breaking up the cinnamon; also put in the juice of a small lemon, one blade of mace, a quarter of a nutmeg grated, and four lumps of sugar that have been rubbed over the skin of a fresh pale-looking lemon. Put a lid on the saucepan, and let these spices boil on the fire gently for half an hour, or a little more. Next take a bottle of port wine, and decant it gently, in case of sediment, in the ordinary way; heat this in a saucepan, *but do not let it boil*; as soon as it is hot, pour the wine into a bowl previously made thoroughly hot with hot water, add the liquor of the spices and lemon-juice through a strainer, place the hot lemon in the bishop, and grate a little fresh nutmeg over the top, and add sufficient sugar to the whole, according to the tastes of the party. Of course, this is a somewhat strong mixture, and is certainly not altogether suited for children in any quantity. However, by adding more boiling water and more sugar it can soon be made weaker. Of course, the proper vessel into which the bishop should be poured is a punch-bowl. Unfortunately, punch-bowls are somewhat rare. If the party is tolerably large, a wash-hand basin makes a very fair substitute. Of course, you would pick a small one, and as ornamental as possible. Now, a thick basin requires a good deal of warming, so should you adopt my suggestion, recollect to fill the basin with boiling water some time before it is wanted. In lieu of a punch-ladle, the soup-ladle will be found a worthy substitute. I would also remind you of warming the glasses, not only for the sake of keeping the bishop hot, but to avoid breakages. In cold weather, especially when it is frosty, pouring any hot liquid into a cold glass is very apt to end in cracking it. The bowl too, should be placed in front of the fire on a hassock in the centre of the family circle.

Mulled claret is made in a very similar manner to bishop, only no roasted lemon is required. Take a small quantity of water, and boil in it for some time the same quantity of cinnamon and mace as recommended for the bishop, but do not put in any lemon juice. After this has boiled for some time, add some white sugar—a dozen lumps or more, for claret requires a far greater amount of sugar than port. After adding the sugar, do not boil up the water and spices, as the addition of the sugar makes it extremely likely to boil over. Next warm a bottle of claret on the fire, taking care, as before, not to let it boil. When it is thoroughly hot, strain off the sweetened and spiced water, and add a little grated nutmeg, and a table-spoonful of pale brandy. If you have a large jug with a strainer in the spout, there is no occasion to strain off the spices. Mulled claret is generally put into a jug, and not into a bowl.

There is a good old-fashioned sound about the "wassail-bowl." I have never tried the following recipe, but will give it, as it sounds fairly correct:—Heat in a saucepan a pint of Burton ale, with half a pound of sugar, a grated nutmeg, and half an ounce of grated ginger; after it has just boiled up, add a quart more ale, four glasses of golden sherry, and a couple of ounces of lump sugar that has been rubbed over the outside of a lemon. Add also a few thin slices of lemon. Make the whole mixture hot without boiling it, and add half a dozen roasted apples that have had the cores stamped out and cut, but that have not been peeled.

Of course, this must be placed in a bowl, which must be treated, as we said, with hot water. The sort of ale that must be used for the wassail-bowl is evidently strong old ale, like Burton or Edinburgh, and I should think the more sweet and oily the ale the better the wassail. Mild ale or bitter ale would not answer, especially the latter.

I have on previous occasions gone into the mysteries of mince pies and plum pudding, as well as into turkey-stuffing and goose-stuffing. How to roast a sirloin of beef, though important, is too well known to warrant many words. There is, however, no season in the year in which cold roast beef is so plentiful as the day after Christmas Day. Now, though cold roast beef really does not want any sauce at all, yet there is one that so admirably suits it that I think it is well worth mentioning at the present season. I refer to horseradish sauce. Horseradish sauce used to be made by mixing together grated horseradish with sugar, mustard, vinegar, and cream. There has, however, been an admirable modern invention called Swiss milk, preserved in tins. When, therefore, you have any compound requiring cream and sugar, by using Swiss milk with ordinary milk you get an exactly similar result, at a far less cost. To make horseradish sauce proceed as follows:—Take a stick or two of horseradish, and send it through a coarse grater till you have sufficient pulp to fill, say, a couple of tablespoons. This grating process, like chopping onions, is far from pleasant, as it makes one cry. Next dissolve about a tea-spoonful of Swiss milk in a little ordinary milk—say two table-spoonfuls of the latter—and mix in about a tea-spoonful of made mustard and a tea-spoonful of vinegar, then mix in the two table-spoonfuls of horseradish pulp, and stir it all together.

The consistency should be that of good thick cream; of course, by adding more pulp the mixture will be rendered thicker. Should it be too sweet, of course it is owing to there being too much Swiss milk, and as Swiss milk is apt to vary somewhat in sweetness, it is as well to act cautiously in using it, as it is always easy to add, but impossible to take away. Some persons, when serving horseradish with hot beef or hot rump steak, warm the sauce; this is a great mistake, as by warming the sauce you utterly spoil it, and to my mind render it absolutely disagreeable.

In speaking of Christmas dinners last year, I mentioned that an exceedingly nice stuffing for turkeys can be made from chestnuts. As anything in connection with turkeys is very *apropos* of the present season, I will describe how to make chestnut stuffing and chestnut sauce. For a large turkey, take about sixty chestnuts and slit the skins, and fry them for a short time in a little butter in a frying-pan till their husks come off easily. Then boil the chestnuts in some good strong stock till quite tender; take one-half and pound it in a mortar, with a little pepper and salt and scraped fat bacon; stuff a turkey with this and an equal quantity of ordinary veal stuffing or sausage-meat.

With regard to the sauce, take the remainder of the chestnuts and mix them with some good strong gravy, rubbing the whole through a wire sieve with a wooden spoon; a couple of lumps of sugar and a glass of sherry are an improvement. Of course, the best stuffing of all for turkeys is made from truffles, but then they are so expensive, as a rule, that the recipe would not be practical.

The Christmas Dinner Party

from

COOKERY FOR
LITTLE GIRLS

BY
OLIVE HYDE FOSTER

NEW YORK
DUFFIELD & COMPANY
MCMX

The Christmas Dinner Party

Our little cook, after her experience at Thanksgiving, will probably be most eager to take part in the preparations for the Christmas dinner. Consult her now, as before; tell her all your ideas, get her suggestions, and then make all plans at least a week beforehand. Holidays should be holidays for the hostess as well as the guest, and can be made so by the choice of a dinner that is good and at the same time easily prepared. The suggested menu following will be found attractive enough for any party, and at the same time it is neither expensive nor very difficult to get ready.

Let the little girl again make out the bill of fare and hang up in the kitchen for reference, make out her list for market and grocery, and help in the selection of the goose, the vegetables and the fruits. Thus she will learn the best kinds to buy and what they cost, and incidentally mother and daughter can have a regular little lark out of the expedition and become better chums than in almost any other way.

CHRISTMAS MENU
MENU FOR CHRISTMAS DINNER

Raw Oysters, Horseradish

Roast Goose   *Apple Sauce*   *Celery*

Mashed Potatoes   *Lima Beans*

Tomato Jelly Salad

Plum Pudding

Fruit   *Nuts*   *Raisins*

Coffee

The first dish to make, strange to say, is the last one on the list, and the plum pudding is better if made several weeks before it is needed, and then simply steamed up again for a couple of hours just before serving. A fine old recipe that had been in a friend's family for years, was once given me, but as it filled six molds I reduced it to the following proportions, which is ample for a mold large enough for eight people:

PLUM PUDDING

One-half cupful butter, three-quarters cupful sugar, one-quarter pound suet, two and one-half cupfuls flour, one-half pound seeded raisins, one-half pound currants, one ounce citron, three eggs yolks and whites (beaten separately), one-half cupful milk, one-quarter cupful almonds (blanched and chopped fine), one-quarter cupful brandy (or boiled cider if preferred), one-half teaspoonful cloves, one-quarter teaspoonful nutmeg, one teaspoonful cinnamon.

After getting all her ingredients out on the table and ready, the little cook should cream her butter and sugar, beat in yolks, add milk, and then stir in the flour alternately with the stiff whites. Then put in the brandy and spice, and last of all the fruit and nuts, dredged with a little flour. This should be well stirred, and then packed in a thoroughly greased covered mold and steamed for four hours.

HARD SAUCE

Two kinds of sauce are nice for this pudding, served together. A hard sauce is made by creaming one-half cupful of butter in one cupful of fine sugar, adding half teaspoonful of brandy or vanilla and one teaspoonful cream and stirring until light and creamy. It can be set in a bowl of hot water at first to help make the butter cream, but after being beaten light should be set in the cold to harden. A teaspoonful of this hard sauce is served on each portion of the pudding.

HOT SAUCE

The following hot sauce is poured around: one-quarter cupful butter, one cupful sugar, one teaspoonful flour. Mix flour and sugar, add butter and one cupful cold water, and stir until it boils and thickens. Flavor with nutmeg.

The day before Christmas repeat the lesson in dressing a fowl, and let her make the stuffing from the recipe used before, only this time she should omit the sage or oysters and season with a small onion chopped fine.

APPLE SAUCE

For the accompanying apple sauce, let her peel and quarter half a dozen tart apples, put on to cook in a cup of cold water, and when tender press through a colander, sweeten to taste, and then put in a pretty glass dish and grate nutmeg over the top. This should then be covered and set away until ready to be carried to the table.

OYSTERS ON THE HALF SHELL

As we intended to have as little work as possible about this particular dinner, I have suggested raw oysters for the first course instead of a soup. Serve on the half-shell if you can get them that way, putting a little chopped ice on each plate to hold the shells in place, giving four or five oysters to each person, and putting one empty shell in the center to hold the horseradish or slice of lemon. If the oysters are opened at the market all you have to do is to see that they are kept on ice until served.

TOMATO JELLY SALAD

For the tomato jelly salad, first boil together until very tender one quart can of tomatoes, one small sliced onion, six cloves, one-half cupful chopped celery. Strain through a jelly bag, season with salt and pepper, and add gelatin which has been dissolving in a few spoonfuls of cold water. As different brands vary, however, study the directions on the box in order to get the right amount to stiffen one quart of jelly.

If the gelatin does not thoroughly melt with the warm tomato juice, set over the fire for a few moments, and then pour into small molds (wine glasses or after-dinner coffee cups will serve nicely), and set away to harden over night. Next morning fix the required number of salad dishes with lettuce leaves or tender cabbage cut in strings, and turn out carefully the molded tomato jelly. Over the top of each drop a large spoonful of thick boiled dressing.

CHRISTMAS DECORATIONS

A pretty idea for a Christmas table is to carry out as fully as possible a color scheme of red and green. The centerpiece, of course, should be of holly, and a novel one it will be if large beautiful pieces are put in the upper part of a double boiler and set out to freeze. I did this once by accident, and when I went for my holly there it was— imbedded in a solid block of ice. The shape of the oat-meal kettle, like a flowerpot, allowed the ice to turn out easily, and it could then be set on a plate and trimmed around the bottom with the holly leaves. A couple of bolts of red baby ribbon will be enough for streamers from the chandelier to each plate, at which should be a pretty piece of the holly—or better still, if you can get them, three or four red carnations for each lady, and one for the buttonhole of each gentleman.

COLOR SCHEME

To carry out this color plan, the oysters should be served with catsup and garnished with parsley, the tomato jelly be turned out on lettuce, the plum pudding (ablaze with a spoonful of alcohol) decorated with holly, and the candy—red and white peppermint wafers—tied with green baby ribbon.

If the details of preparing the dinner have been followed out as I have suggested, and everything

possible done the day before, on Christmas
morning there will be little to do: the goose to put
into the oven and roast, the potatoes to mash and
the beans to dress, the plum pudding to heat up,
the sauce to prepare, with the gravy and the
coffee to make at the last moment. Our small
cook of course has the celery cleaned preparatory
to cutting up, and the nuts all cracked, and she
can tie up the candy and assist with the
decorations. Having helped set the table for the
Thanksgiving party, she will feel perfectly
competent to undertake the arrangement now,
alone, and you, Mother, can say, "You have
gotten along with everything so nicely, and
remembered so well, I will let you put on the
dishes and silver all by yourself." Then when she
reports that all is ready, look over the work
yourself and see that it is all right. Possibly she
will have misplaced some pieces, forgotten
others, but if you point out the errors and have
her remedy the mistakes herself, she will likely
remember next time and make her table a well-
appointed one.

Delicious Home-Made Candies

All children love to make candy, and the
home-made kinds are much purer and better—
besides being much cheaper—than those usually
sold at the small confectionery stores. Every
mother will do well to help her little daughter
master this branch of cookery, for it will not only

enable her to make wholesome sweets for the family when desired, but also to prepare a dainty box when she wishes to make an inexpensive present.

NUT CANDY

For fine nut candy, have the child first pick out half a cupful of nut meats. Put on in a small saucepan two level cupfuls of light-brown sugar, one-half cupful of water, a level teaspoonful of butter and a tablespoonful of vinegar, and boil without stirring until the candy crackles when dropped in cold water. Pour into a well-buttered pie-pan that has been sprinkled with the nuts, and as soon as cool, mark into squares.

MAPLE FUDGE

For delicious maple fudge, take one and one-half cupfuls of light-brown sugar, one cupful of maple sirup, half a cupful of milk, and a level teaspoonful of butter. Boil slowly until it makes a soft ball when rolled between the fingers in cold water, then set aside until cool. Then beat with a fork until a creamy, sugary mass, turn quickly on to a buttered plate and mark into squares. If the little cook finds it is soft from having been taken off a moment too soon, she will have to let it stand longer to turn to sugar, but the fudge that stands overnight will be particularly smooth.

CREAM CANDY

Cream candy is made by boiling two cupfuls of granulated sugar, *without stirring*, with three-fourths cupful water, two tablespoonfuls vinegar and a teaspoonful of butter until brittle when dropped in cold water. Pour on to a buttered pan, but do not scrape the sugared edge of the kettle, and pull as soon as cool. If a little care is exercised in handling at first, it will not stick to the fingers. The butter or flour sometimes put on the hands to prevent this only spoils the candy. When pulled perfectly white, cut with scissors into small cubes. The longer this stands, the more delicious it becomes, and if flavored with a few drops of essence of peppermint when first put on (so it can be well stirred through) and then put away when done in a glass jar for a couple of weeks, it will make delicate "after-dinner mint."

CHOCOLATE CREAMS

Easy chocolate creams require two cupfuls of confectioner's sugar, with a few teaspoonfuls of milk to moisten enough to work like dough, and a quarter teaspoonful of vanilla. Knead well, and work out into small balls. Melt one square of unsweetened chocolate by first grating and then setting in a pan of hot water, and drop in the creams, one at a time. Roll around quickly with a fork, and lift on to a sheet of buttered paper. Put in a cool place to harden. Different flavorings can be used instead of all vanilla, and half an English walnut stuck on the top of each cream before the chocolate hardens will add to the attractiveness. Or, instead of dipping all the creams in the chocolate, they can be cut in half and wrapped around with figs or seeded dates. They will grow more creamy if allowed to stand a day or two.

FUDGE

Particularly smooth fudge is made in a way that seems strange until you try it. Take two cups of sugar, half a cup of milk, one tablespoonful of butter, a few drops of vanilla, and four tablespoonfuls of cocoa. Mix, and boil without stirring until it makes a soft ball when dropped in cold water. Remove from the fire, set aside until cool, then pour on to a buttered platter and beat with a silver fork until creamy. When you see it beginning to harden, quickly smooth out and mark in squares.

MOLASSES TAFFY

All little children like this, and it is easily made. To two cups of molasses, add one cup of sugar, two tablespoons of butter, and boil until brittle when dropped in cold water. Add then one-fourth teaspoonful of soda, stir through and pour on buttered tins. When cool enough to handle pull to a light color, cut in sticks, and lay on oiled paper to harden. This is good flavored with a few drops of peppermint, but do not get in too much.

STUFFED DATES

Stuffed dates are a most wholesome sweet, and quickly made, too. The dates must first be picked apart, washed in warm water and dried in an old napkin. Remove the seed from each with a sharp knife, slip a nut in its place, press together, and sift over with granulated sugar. Leave standing a while on oiled paper to become firm. They are nice served at the end of a dinner, with the dessert and coffee.

SALTED NUTS

Salted nuts, used so much, are usually placed on the table when it is set, and passed during the meal. They are very expensive if bought ready for use, but quite inexpensive made at home. Either almonds or peanuts can be used, but the almonds must first be dropped in boiling water long enough to loosen the skins, which will slip off easily in a cloth. Melt half a teaspoonful of butter in a pie-pan, pour in a cup of nut meats, stir enough to cover with the oil, and brown in the oven. Remove, and rub dry with a soft cloth, and sprinkle with fine salt.

Our Very Happy Christmas

from

Letters of a Woman Homesteader

By Elinore P. Stewart

1910

Elinore Stewart was a homesteader in Wyoming. From 1909 to 1914, she wrote a series of letters to a friend in Colorado, describing her new life in Wyoming. These letters were later published. The following letter tells of a very special Christmas.

January 6, 1913

My dear Friend,—

I have put off writing you and thanking you for your thought for us until now so that I could tell you of our very happy Christmas and our deer hunt all at once.

To begin with, Mr. Stewart and Junior have gone to Boulder to spend the winter. Clyde wanted his mother to have a chance to enjoy our boy, so, as he had to go, he took Junior with him. Then those of my dear neighbors nearest my heart decided to prevent a lonely Christmas for me, so on December 21st came Mrs. Louderer, laden with an immense plum pudding and a big "wurst," and a little later came Mrs. O'Shaughnessy on her frisky pony, Chief, her scarlet sweater making a bright bit of color against our snow-wrapped horizon. Her face and ways are just as bright and cheery as can be. When she saw Mrs. Louderer's pudding and sausage she said she had brought nothing because she had come to get something to eat herself, "and," she continued, "it is a private opinion of mine that my neighbors are so glad to see me that they are glad to feed me." Now wouldn't that little speech have made her welcome anywhere?

Well, we were hilariously planning what Mrs. O'Shaughnessy called a "widdy" Christmas and getting supper, when a great stamping-off of snow proclaimed a newcomer. It was Gavotte, and we were powerfully glad to see him because the hired man was going to a dance and we knew Gavotte would contrive some unusual amusement. He had heard that Clyde was going to have a deer-drive, and didn't know that he had gone, so he had come down to join the hunt just for the fun, and was very much disappointed to find there was going to be no hunt. After supper, however, his good humor returned and he told us story after story of big hunts he had had in Canada. He worked up his own enthusiasm as well as ours, and at last proposed that we have a drive of our own for a Christmas "joy." He said he would take a station and do the shooting if one of us would do the driving. So right now I reckon I had better tell you how it is done.

There are many little parks in the mountains where the deer can feed, although now most places are so deep in snow that they can't walk in it. For that reason they have trails to water and to the different feeding-grounds, and they can't get through the snow except along these paths. You see how easy it would be for a man hidden on the trail to get one of the beautiful creatures if some one coming from another direction startled them so that they came along that particular path.

So they made their plans. Mrs.
O'Shaughnessy elected herself driver. Two miles
away is a huge mountain called Phillipeco, and
deer were said to be plentiful up there. At one
time there had been a sawmill on the mountain,
and there were a number of deserted cabins in
which we could make ourselves comfortable. So
it was planned that we go up the next morning,
stay all night, have the hunt the following
morning, and then come home with our game.

Well, we were all astir early the next
morning and soon grain, bedding, and chuck-box
were in the wagon. Then Mrs. Louderer, the
kinder, and myself piled in; Mrs. O'Shaughnessy
bestrode Chief, Gavotte stalked on ahead to pick
our way, and we were off.

It was a long, tedious climb, and I wished
over and over that I had stayed at home; but it
was altogether on Baby's account. I was so
afraid that he would suffer, but he kept warm as
toast. The day was beautiful, and the views
many times repaid us for any hardship we had
suffered. It was three o'clock before we reached
the old mill camp. Soon we had a roaring fire,
and Gavotte made the horses comfortable in one
of the cabins. They were bedded in soft, dry
sawdust, and were quite as well off as if they
had been in their own stalls. Then some rough
planks were laid on blocks, and we had our first
meal since breakfast. We called it supper, and
we had potatoes roasted in the embers, Mrs.

Louderer's wurst, which she had been calmly carrying around on her arm like a hoop and which was delicious with the bread that Gavotte toasted on long sticks; we had steaming coffee, and we were all happy; even Baby clapped his hands and crowed at the unusual sight of an open fire. After supper Gavotte took a little stroll and returned with a couple of grouse for our breakfast. After dark we sat around the fire eating peanuts and listening to Gavotte and Mrs. Louderer telling stories of their different great forests. But soon Gavotte took his big sleeping-bag and retired to another cabin, warning us that we must be up early. Our improvised beds were the most comfortable things; I love the flicker of an open fire, the smell of the pines, the pure, sweet air, and I went to sleep thinking how blest I was to be able to enjoy the things I love most.

It seemed only a short time until some one knocked on our door and we were all wide awake in a minute. The fire had burned down and only a soft, indistinct glow from the embers lighted the room, while through a hole in the roof I could see a star glimmering frostily. It was Gavotte at the door and he called through a crack saying he had been hearing queer noises for an hour and he was going to investigate. He had called us so that we need not be alarmed should we hear the noise and not find him. We scrambled into our clothes quickly and ran outdoors to listen.

I can never describe to you the weird beauty of a moonlight night among the pines when the snow is sparkling and gleaming, the deep silence unbroken even by the snapping of a twig. We stood shivering and straining our ears and were about to go back to bed when we heard faintly a long-drawn wail as if all the suffering and sorrow on earth were bound up in that one sound. We couldn't tell which way it came from; it seemed to vibrate through the air and chill our hearts. I had heard that panthers cried that way, but Gavotte said it was not a panther. He said the engine and saws had been moved from where we were to another spring across the cañon a mile away, where timber for sawing was more plentiful, but he supposed every one had left the mill when the water froze so they couldn't saw. He added that some one must have remained and was, perhaps, in need of help, and if we were not afraid he would leave us and go see what was wrong.

We went in, made up the fire, and sat in silence, wondering what we should see or hear next. Once or twice that agonized cry came shivering through the cold moonlight. After an age, we heard Gavotte crunching through the snow, whistling cheerily to reassure us. He had crossed the cañon to the new mill camp, where he had found two women, loggers' wives, and some children. One of the women, he said, was "so ver' seek," 't was she who was wailing so, and it was the kind of "seek" where we could be of every help and comfort.

150

Mrs. Louderer stayed and took care of the children while Mrs. O'Shaughnessy and I followed after Gavotte, panting and stumbling, through the snow. Gavotte said he suspected they were short of "needfuls," so he had filled his pockets with coffee and sugar, took in a bottle some of the milk I brought for Baby, and his own flask of whiskey, without which he never travels.

At last, after what seemed to me hours of scrambling through the snow, through deepest gloom where pines were thickest, and out again into patches of white moonlight, we reached the ugly clearing where the new camp stood. Gavotte escorted us to the door and then returned to our camp. Entering, we saw the poor, little soon-to-be mother huddled on her poor bed, while an older woman stood near warning her that the oil would soon be all gone and they would be in darkness. She told us that the sick one had been in pain all the day before and much of the night, and that she herself was worn completely out. So Mrs. O'Shaughnessy sent her to bed and we took charge.

Secretly, I felt it all to be a big nuisance to be dragged out from my warm, comfortable bed to traipse through the snow at that time of the night. But the moment poor little Molly spoke I was glad I was living, because she was a poor little Southern girl whose husband is a Mormon. He had been sent on a mission to Alabama, and

the poor girl had fallen in love with his
handsome face and knew nothing of
Mormonism, so she had run away with him. She
thought it would be so grand to live in the
glorious West with so splendid a man as she
believed her husband to be. But now she
believed she was going to die and she was glad
of it because she could not return to her "folks,"
and she said she knew her husband was dead
because he and the other woman's husband,
both of whom had intended to stay there all
winter and cut logs, had gone two weeks before
to get their summer's wages and buy supplies.
Neither man had come back and there was not a
horse or any other way to get out of the
mountains to hunt them, so they believed the
men to be frozen somewhere on the road. Rather
a dismal prospect, wasn't it? Molly was just
longing for some little familiar thing, so I was
glad I have not yet gotten rid of my Southern
way of talking. No Westerner can ever
understand a Southerner's need of sympathy,
and, however kind their hearts, they are unable
to give it. Only a Southerner can understand
how dear are our peculiar words and phrases,
and poor little Molly took new courage when she
found I knew what she meant when she said she
was just "honin'" after a friendly voice.

Well, soon we had the water hot and had
filled some bottles and placed them around our
patient, and after a couple of hours the tiny
little stranger came into the world. It had been
necessary to have a great fire in order to have

152

light, so as soon as we got Baby dressed I opened the door a little to cool the room and Molly saw the morning star twinkling merrily. "Oh," she said, "that is what I will call my little girlie,—Star, dear little Star."

It is strange, isn't it? how our spirits will revive after some great ordeal. Molly had been sure she was going to die and saw nothing to live for; now that she had had a cup of hot milk and held her red little baby close, she was just as happy and hopeful as if she had never left her best friends and home to follow the uncertain fortunes of young Will Crosby. So she and I talked of ash-hoppers, smoke-houses, cotton-patches, goobers, poke-greens, and shoats, until she fell asleep.

Soon day was abroad, and so we went outdoors for a fresh breath. The other woman came out just then to ask after Molly. She invited us into her cabin, and, oh, the little Mormons were everywhere; poor, half-clad little things! Some sour-dough biscuit and a can of condensed milk was everything they had to eat. The mother explained to us that their "men" had gone to get things for them, but had not come back, so she guessed they had got drunk and were likely in jail. She told it in a very unconcerned manner. Poor thing! Years of such experience had taught her that blessed are they who expect nothing, for they shall not be disappointed. She said that if Molly had not been sick she would have walked down out of the mountains and got help.

Just then two shots rang out in quick succession, and soon Gavotte came staggering along with a deer across his shoulders. That he left for the family. From our camp he had brought some bacon and butter for Molly, and, poor though it may seem, it was a treat for her. Leaving the woman to dress the venison with her oldest boy's aid, we put out across the cañon for our own breakfast. Beside our much-beaten trail hung the second venison, and when we reached our camp and had our own delicious breakfast of grouse, bread, butter, and coffee, Gavotte took Chub and went for our venison. In a short time we were rolling homeward. Of course it didn't take us nearly so long to get home because it was downhill and the road was clearly marked, so in a couple of hours we were home.

Gavotte knew the two loggers were in Green River and were then at work storing ice for the railroad, but he had not known that their wives were left as they were. The men actually had got drunk, lost their money, and were then trying to replace it. After we debated a bit we decided we could not enjoy Christmas with those people in want up there in the cold. Then we got busy. It is sixty miles to town, although our nearest point to the railroad is but forty, so you see it was impossible to get to town to get anything.

You should have seen us! Every old garment that had ever been left by men who have worked here was hauled out, and Mrs. O'Shaughnessy's deft fingers soon had a pile of garments cut. We kept the machine humming until far into the night, as long as we could keep our eyes open.

All next day we sewed as hard as we could, and Gavotte cooked as hard as he could. We had intended to have a tree for Jerrine, so we had a box of candles and a box of Christmas snow. Gavotte asked for all the bright paper we could find. We had lots of it, and I think you would be surprised at the possibilities of a little waste paper. He made gorgeous birds, butterflies, and flowers out of paper that once wrapped parcels. Then he asked us for some silk thread, but I had none, so he told us to comb our hair and give him the combings. We did, and with a drop of mucilage he would fasten a hair to a bird's back and then hold it up by the hair. At a few feet's distance it looked exactly as though the bird was flying. I was glad I had a big stone jar full of fondant, because we had a lot of fun shaping and coloring candies. Mrs. Louderer cut up her big plum pudding and put it into a dozen small bags. These Gavotte carefully covered with green paper. Then we tore up the holly wreath that Aunt Mary sent me, and put a sprig in the top of each green bag of pudding. I never had so much fun in my life as I had preparing for that Christmas.

At ten o'clock, the morning of the 24th, we were again on our way up the mountain-side. We took shovels so we could clear a road if need be. We had dinner at the old camp, and then Gavotte hunted us a way out to the new, and we smuggled our things into Molly's cabin so the children should have a real surprise. Poor, hopeless little things! Theirs was, indeed, a dull outlook.

Gavotte busied himself in preparing one of the empty cabins for us and in making the horses comfortable. He cut some pine boughs to do that with, and so they paid no attention when he cut a small tree. In the mean time we had cleared everything from Molly's cabin but her bed; we wanted her to see the fun. The children were sent to the spring to water the horses and they were all allowed to ride, so that took them out of the way while Gavotte nailed the tree into a box he had filled with dirt to hold it steady.

There were four women of us, and Gavotte, so it was only the work of a few moments to get the tree ready, and it was the most beautiful one I ever saw. Your largest bell, dear Mrs. Coney, dangled from the topmost branch. Gavotte had attached a long, stout wire to your Santa Claus, so he was able to make him dance frantically without seeming to do so. The hairs that held the birds and butterflies could not be seen, and the effect was beautiful. We had a bucket of apples rubbed bright, and these we fastened to the tree just as they grew on their own branches. The puddings looked pretty, too, and we had done up the parcels that held the clothes as attractively as we could. We saved the candy and the peanuts to put in their little stockings.

As soon as it was dark we lighted the candles and then their mother called the children. Oh, if you could have seen them! It was the very first Christmas tree they had ever seen and they didn't know what to do. The very first present Gavotte handed out was a pair of trousers for eight-years-old Brig, but he just stood and stared at the tree until his brother next in size, with an eye to the main chance, got behind him and pushed him forward, all the time exclaiming, "Go on, can't you! They ain't doin' nothin' to you, they's just doin' somethin' for you." Still Brig would not put out his hand. He just shook his tousled sandy head and said he wanted a bird. So the fun kept up for an hour. Santa had for Molly a package of oatmeal, a pound of butter, a Mason jar of cream, and a dozen eggs, so that she could have suitable food to eat until something could be done.

After the presents had all been distributed we put the phonograph on a box and had a dandy concert. We played "There were Shepherds," "Ave Maria," and "Sweet Christmas Bells." Only we older people cared for those, so then we had "Arrah Wanna," "Silver Bells," "Rainbow," "Red Wing," and such songs. How delighted they were! Our concert lasted two hours, and by that time the little fellows were so sleepy that the excitement no longer affected them and they were put to bed, but they hung up their stockings first, and even Molly hung hers up too. We filled them with peanuts and candy.

Next morning the happiness broke out in new spots. The children were all clean and warm, though I am afraid I can't brag on the fit of all the clothes. But the pride of the wearers did away with the necessity of a fit. The mother was radiantly thankful for a warm petticoat; that it was made of a blanket too small for a bed didn't bother her, and the stripes were around the bottom anyway. Molly openly rejoiced in her new gown, and that it was made of ugly gray outing flannel she didn't know nor care. Baby Star Crosby looked perfectly sweet in her little new clothes, and her little gown had blue sleeves and they thought a white skirt only added to its beauty. And so it was about everything. We all got so much out of so little. I will never again allow even the smallest thing to go to waste. We were every one just as happy as we could be, and there was very little given that had not been thrown away or was not just odds and ends.

There was never anything more true than that it is more blessed to give than to receive. We certainly had a delicious dinner too, and we let Molly have all she wanted that we dared allow her to eat. The roast venison was so good that we were tempted to let her taste it, but we thought better of that. As soon as dinner was over we packed our belongings and betook ourselves homeward.

It was just dusk when we reached home. Away off on a bare hill a wolf barked. A big owl hooted lonesomely among the pines, and soon a pack of yelping coyotes went scampering across the frozen waste.

It was not the Christmas I had in mind when I sent the card, but it was a dandy one, just the same.

With best wishes for you for a happy, happy
New Year,
Sincerely your friend,
Elinore Rupert Stewart

The Cowboy's Christmas Ball

Poem by
Larry Chittenden

1890

The Cowboy's Christmas Ball began in 1885 in Anson, Texas. It was an annual tradition at the Star Hotel until 1889, when the hotel burned down. But the ball (and the town) made such an impression on a guest named Larry Chittenden that he composed a poem about it. The poem took on a life of its own, and was subsequently published in at least two books of song and poetry.

160

The Cowboy's Christmas Ball

'Way out in Western Texas, where the Clear
Fork's waters flow,
Where the cattle are "a-browzin'," an' the
Spanish ponies grow;
Where the Northers "come a-whistlin'" from
beyond the Neutral Strip;
And the prairie dogs are sneezin', as if they had
"The Grip";
Where the cayotes come a-howlin' 'round the
ranches after dark,
And the mocking-birds are singin' to the lovely
"medder lark";
Where the 'possum and the badger, and
rattlesnakes abound,
And the monstrous stars are winkin' o'er a
wilderness profound;
Where lonesome, tawny prairies melt into airy
streams,
While the Double Mountains slumber, in
heavenly kinds of dreams;
Where the antelope is grazin' and the lonely
plovers call—
It was there that I attended "The Cowboys'
Christmas Ball."
The town was Anson City, old Jones's county
seat,
Where they raised Polled Angus cattle, and
waving whiskered wheat;
Where the air is soft and "bammy," an' dry an'
full of health,

And the prairies is explodin' with agricultural
wealth;
Where they print the Texas Western, that Hec.
McCann supplies
With news and yarns and stories, uv most
amazin' size;
Where Frank Smith "pulls the badger," on
knowin' tenderfeet,
And Democracy's triumphant, and might hard
to beat;
Where lives that good old hunter, John Milsap,
from Lamar,
Who "used to be the Sheriff, back East, in Paris
sah!"
'T was there, I say, at Anson with the lovely
"widder Wall,"
That I went to that reception, "The Cowboys'
Christmas Ball."
The boys had left the ranches and come to town
in piles;
The ladies—"kinder scatterin'"— had gathered
in for miles.
And yet the place was crowded, as I remember
well,
'T was got for the occasion, at "The Morning
Star Hotel.
The music was a fiddle an' a lively tambourine,
And a "viol came imported," by the stage from
Abilene.
The room was togged out gorgeous-with
mistletoe and shawls,
And candles flickered frescoes, around the airy
walls.

The "wimmin folks" looked lovely-the boys
looked kinder treed,
Till their leader commenced yellin': "Whoa!
fellers, let's stampede,"
And the music started sighin', an' awailin'
through the hall
As a kind of introduction to "The Cowboys'
Christmas Ball."
The leader was a feller that came from
Swenson's ranch,
They called him "Windy Billy," from "little
Deadman's Branch."
His rig was "kinder keerless," big spurs and
high-heeled boots;
He had the reputation that comes when "fellers
shoots."
His voice was like a bugle upon the mountain's
height;
His feet were animated an' a mighty, movin'
sight,
When he commenced to holler, "Neow, fellers
stake your pen!
"Lock horns ter all them heifers, an' russle 'em
like men.
"Saloot yer lovely critters; neow swing an' let
'em go,
"Climb the grape vine 'round 'em—all hands do-
ce-do!
"You Mavericks, jine the round-up- Jest skip her
waterfall,"
Huh! hit wuz gettin' happy, "The Cowboys'
Christmas Ball!"
The boys were tolerable skittish, the ladies
powerful neat,

That old bass viol's music just got there with both feet!
That wailin', frisky fiddle, I never shall forget;
And Windy kept a-singin'-I think I hear him yet-
"Oh Xes, chase yer squirrels, an' cut 'em to one side;
"Spur Treadwell to the centre, with Cross P Charley's bride;
"Doc. Hollis down the middle, an' twine the ladies' chain;
"Varn Andrews pen the fillies in big T Diamond's train.
"All pull yer freight together, neow swallow fork an' change;
"'Big Boston,' lead the trail herd, through little Pitchfork's range.
"Purr 'round yer gentle pussies, neow rope 'em! Balance all!"
Huh! hit wuz gettin' active-"The Cowboys' Christmas Ball!"
The dust riz fast an' furious; we all jes' galloped 'round,
Till the scenery got so giddy that T Bar Dick was downed.
We buckled to our partners, an' told 'em to hold on,
Then shook our hoofs like lightning, until the early dawn.
Don't tell me 'bout cotillions, or germans. No sire 'ee!
That whirl at Anson City just takes the cake with me.
I'm sick of lazy shufflin's, of them I've had my fill,

Give me a frontier break-down, backed up by Windy Bill.
McAllister ain't nowhar: when Windy leads the show,
I've seen 'em both in harness, and so I sorter know—
Oh, Bill, I sha'n't forget yer, and I'll oftentimes recall,
That lively gaited sworray—"The Cowboys' Christmas Ball."

Letter from a Civil War soldier

Richard H. Greene, the only known black Civil War surgeon to serve with the Navy during the (Civil) war.

Dear Mother,

I received last evening a letter from you, dated the 15th, which I consider my Christmas, and it is indeed a very acceptable one to I assume you. For if I am deprived the pleasure of being at home on this day, you can imagine me sitting by a fire in the chimney reading over your letter again and again, which caused my mind and especially on this day to wander and dwell homeward as to our family affairs, and wish I was so situated that I could drop in often for a few hours at least, and receive the benefit of counsel together, for I sometimes feel – and in fact I am – dependent on my own exertions for success in this world (not for a moment forgetting the assistance I have always received at home) but you understand me when I mean the counsel of Father or older Brother, who have had experience in the ways of the world.

Christmas on the Rappahannock

By Rev. John R. Paxton, D.D.

1862

"Gentlemen, the chair of the Professor of the Mathematics is vacant in this college; permit me to introduce to you Captain Fraser." Rah! rah! rah! and away we went and enlisted – to go to Richmond. It took us three years to get there. No wonder; there were so many Longstreets to make our way through; so many Hills to climb; so many Stonewalls to batter down; so many Picketts to clear out of the way. It was as hard as a road to travel as the steep and stony one to heaven.

No preaching, sir! Can't you forget the shop? Don't you know that you have squeezed yourself into that faded, jacket, and are squirming, with a flushed face and short breaths, behind that sword belt, which had caused a rebellion *in media res?*

I started for Richmond in July, 1862, a lad eighteen years old, a junior in college, and chafing to be at it, – to double quick it after John Brown's soul, which, since it did not require a knapsack or three days' rations or a canteen or a halt during the night for sleep, was always marching on. On the night before Christmas, 1862, I was a dejected young patriot, wishing I hadn't done it, shivering in the open weather a mile back of the Rappahannock, on the reserve picket and exposed to a wet snowstorm. There was not a stick of wood within five miles of us; all cut down, down, even the roots of trees, and burned up. We lay down on our rubber blankets, pulled our woolen blankets over us, spooned it as close as we could to get to steal warmth from our comrades and tried not to cry.

Next morning the snow lay heavy and deep, and the men, when I wakened and looked about me, reminded me of a church graveyard in winter. "Fall in for picket duty. There, come, Moore, McMeaus, Paxton, Perrine, Pollock, fall in." We fell in, of course, No breakfast; chilled to the marrow; snow a foot deep. We tightened our belts on our empty stomachs, seized our rifles and marched to the river to take our six hours on duty.

It was Christmas Day, 1862. "And so this is war," my old me said to himself while he paced in the snow his two hours on the river's brink. "And I am out here to shoot that lean, lank, coughing, cadaverous-looking butternut fellow over the river. So this is war; this is being a soldier; this is the genuine article; this is H. Greely's 'On to Richmond.' Well, I wish he were here in my place, running to keep warm, pounding his arms and breast to make the chilled blood circulate. So this is war, tramping up and down this river my fifty yards with wet feet, empty stomach, swollen nose."

Alas, when lying under the trees in the college campus last June, war meant to me martial music, gorgeous brigadiers in blue and gold, tall young men in line, shining in brass. War meant to me tumultuous memories of

Bunker Hill, Caesar's Tenth Legion, the Charge of the Six Hundred, – anything but this. Pshaw, I wish I were home. Let me see. Home? God's country. A tear? Yes, it is a tear. What are they doing at home? This is Christmas Day. Home? Well, stockings on the wall, candy, turkey, fun, merry Christmas, and the face of the girl I left behind. Another tear? Yes, I couldn't help it. I was only eighteen, and there was such a contrast between Christmas, 1862, on the Rappahannock and other Christmases. Yes, there was a girl, too, – such sweet eyes, such long lashes, such a low tender voice.

"Come, move quicker. Who goes there?" Shift the rifle from one aching shoulder to the other.

"Hello, Johnny, what are you up to?" The river was narrow, but deep and swift. It was a wet cold, not a freezing cold. There was no ice, too swift for that.

"Yank, with no overcoat, shoes full of holes, nothing to eat but parched corn and tabacco, and with this derned Yankee snow a foot deep, there's nothin' left, nothin' but to get up a cough by way of protestin' against this infernal ill treatment of the body. We uns, Yank, all have a cough over here, and there's no sayin' which will run us to hole first, the cough or your bullets."

The snow still fell, the keen wind, raw and fierce, cut to the bone. It was God's worst weather, in God's forlornest, bleakest spot of ground, that Christmas Day of '62 on the Rappahannock, a half-mile below the town of Fredericksburg. But come, pick up your prostrate pluck, you shivering private. Surely there is enough dampness around without your adding to it your tears.

"Let's laugh, boys."

"Hello, Johnny."

"Hello, yourself, Yank."

"Merry Christmas, Johnny."

"Same to you, Yank."

"Say, Johnny, got anything to trade?"

"Say, Johnny, got anything to trade?"

"Parched corn and tabacco, – the size of our Christmas, Yank."

"All right; you shall have some of our coffee and sugar and pork. Boys, find the boats."

Such boats! I see the children sailing them on small lakes in our Central park. Some Yankee, desperately hungry for tobacco, invented them for trading with the Johnnies. They were hid away under the backs of the river for successive relays of pickets.

We got out the boats. An old handkerchief answered for a sail. We loaded them with coffee, sugar, pork, and set the sail and watched them slowly creep to the other shore. And the Johnnies? To see them crowd the bank and push and scramble to be the first to seize the boats, going into the water and stretching out their long arms. Then, when they pulled the boats ashore, and stood in a group over the cargo, and to hear their exclamations, "Hurrah for hog." "Say, that's not roasted rye, but genuine coffee. Smell it, you'uns." "And sugar, too!"

Then they divided the consignment. They laughed and shouted, "Reckon you'uns been good to we'uns this Christmas Day, Yanks." Then they put parched corn, tobacco, ripe persimmons, into the boats and sent them back to us. And we chewed the parched corn, smoked real Virginia leaf, ate persimmons, which if they weren't very filling at least contracted our stomachs to the size of our Christmas dinner. And so the day passed. We shouted, "Merry Christmas, Johnny." They shouted, "Same to you, Yank." And we forgot the biting wind, the chilling cold; we forgot those men over there were our enemies, whom it might be our duty to shoot before evening.

We had bridged the river, spanned the bloody chasm. We were brothers, not foes, waving salutations of good-will in the name of the Babe of Bethlehem, on Christmas Day in '62. At the very front of the opposing armies, the Christ Child struck a truce of us, broke down the wall of partition, became our peace. We exchanged gifts. We shouted greetings back and forth. We kept Christmas and our hears were lighter of it, and our shivering bodes were not quite so cold.

—*Christmas Number, Harper's Weekly, 1886.*

Christmas memories

of

Caroline Richards Clarke

1853, 1857

As published in

Diary of a New York Girl

By Knowledge Keepers Bookstore

November 22, 1853

This is my composition which I wrote: "Which of
the seasons is the pleasantest? Grim winter with
its cold snows and whistling winds, or pleasant
spring with its green grass and budding trees, or
warm summer with its ripening fruit and
beautiful flowers, or delightful autumn with its
golden fruit and splendid sunsets? I think that I
like all the seasons very well. In winter comes the
blazing fire and Christmas treat. Then we can
have sleigh-rides and play in the snow and
generally get pretty cold noses and toses.

December 25, 1853

Uncle Edward Richards sent us a basket of
lovely things from New York for Christmas.
Books and dresses for Anna and me, a
kaleidoscope, large cornucopias of candy, and
games, one of them being battledore and
shuttlecock. Grandmother says we will have to
wait until spring to play it, as it takes so much
room. I wish all the little girls in the world had an
Uncle Edward.

Christmas, 1857

Grandfather and Grandmother do not care much about making Christmas presents. They say, when they were young no one observed Christmas or New Years, but they always kept Thanksgiving day. Our cousins, the Fields and Carrs, gave us several presents and Uncle Edward sent us a basket full from New York by express. Aunt Ann gave me one of the Lucy books and a Franconia story book and to Anna, "The Child's Book on Repentance." When Anna saw the title, she whispered to me and said if she had done anything she was sorry for she was willing to be forgiven. I am afraid she will never read hers but I will lend her mine. Miss Lucy Ellen Guernsey, of Rochester, gave me "Christmas Earnings" and wrote in it, "Carrie C. Richards with the love of the author." I think that is very nice.

December 23, 1859

We have had a Christmas tree and many other attractions in Seminary chapel. The day scholars and townspeople were permitted to participate and we had a post office and received letters from our friends. Mr. E. M. Morse wrote me a fictitious one, claiming to be written from the north pole ten years hence.   I will copy it in my journal for I may lose the letter. I had some gifts on the Christmas tree and gave some. I presented my teacher, Mr. Chubbuck, with two large hemstitched handkerchiefs with his initials embroidered in a corner of each. As he is favored with the euphonious name of Frank Emery Robinson Chubbuck it was a work of art to make his initials look beautiful. I inclosed a stanza in rhyme:

> Amid the changing scenes of life
>   If any storm should rise,
> May you ever have a handkerchief
>   To wipe your weeping eyes.

Here is Mr. Morse's letter:

"*NORTH POLE, 10 January 1869.*

"*MISS CARRIE RICHARDS,*

"*MY DEAR YOUNG FRIEND.—It is very cold here and the pole is covered with ice. I climbed it yesterday to take an observation and arrange our flag, the Stars and Stripes, which I hoisted immediately on my arrival here, ten years ago. I thought I should freeze and the pole was so slippery that I was in great danger of coming down faster than was comfortable. Although this pole has been used for more than 6,000 years it is still as good as new. The works of the Great Architect do not wear out. It is now ten years since I have seen you and my other two Christian Graces and I have no doubt of your present position among the most brilliant, noble and excellent women in all America. I always knew and recognized your great abilities. Nature was very generous to you all and you were enjoying fine advantages at the time I last knew you. I thought your residence with your Grandparents an admirable school for you, and you and your sister were most evidently the best joy of their old age. You certainly owe much to them. At the time that I left my three Christian Graces, Mrs. Grundy was sometimes malicious enough to say that they were injuring themselves by flirting. I always told the old lady that I had the utmost confidence in the judgment and discretion of my pupils and that they would be very careful and prudent in all their conduct. I confessed that flirting was wrong and very injurious to any one who was guilty of it, but I was very sure that you were not. I could not believe that you would disappoint us all and become only ordinary women, but that you would become the most exalted characters, scorning all things unworthy of ladies and Christians and I was right and Mrs. Grundy was wrong. When the ice around the pole thaws out I shall make a flying visit to Canandaigua. I send you a tame polar bear for a playfellow. This letter will be conveyed to you by Esquimaux express.—Most truly yours,*

E. M. MORSE."

I think some one must have shown some verses that we girls wrote, to Mrs. Grundy and made her think that our minds were more upon the young men than they were upon our studies, but if people knew how much time we spent on Paley's "Evidences of Christianity" and Butler's

179

Analogy and Kames' Elements of Criticism and Tytler's Ancient History and Olmstead's Mathematical Astronomy and our French and Latin and arithmetic and algebra and geometry and trigonometry and bookkeeping, they would know we had very little time to think of the masculine gender.

We hope you have enjoyed the various glimpses of Christmas in America across the centuries! This volume is the first in an annual series.

Please visit us at KnowledgeKeepersBookstore.com to see all of our firsthand accounts of American history:

1. Christopher Columbus: His Story and His Journals
2. Valiant Navigators: Sailor's Narratives Of voyages along the New England Coast 1524–1624
3. Miles Standish, the Puritan Captain
4. The First Year at Plymouth Plantation: MOURT'S RELATION A Journal of the Pilgrims at Plymouth
5. Prelude to Independence: The Life of George Washington, Volume 1
6. War in the Colonies: The Life of George Washington, Volume 2
7. Virginia Tutor: Journal of Philip Vickers Fithian
8. Able and Mighty Men: A Biography of the Signers of the Declaration of Independence, and of Washington and Patrick Henry
9. The Iroquois Handbook: History, Manners, and Customs of the Indian Nations Who Once Inhabited Pennsylvania and the Neighbouring States
10. True Stories of Nebraska Pioneers
11. Diary of a New York Girl: Caroline Richards Clarke

Made in the USA
Las Vegas, NV
30 November 2023

81840055R00108